A GUIDE

TO SPIRITUAL LIFE

Swami Brahmananda (1863–1922)

A GUIDE TO SPIRITUAL LIFE

SPIRITUAL TEACHINGS OF SWAMI BRAHMANANDA

Translated with a Biographical Introduction by
Swami Chetanananda

VEDANTA SOCIETY OF ST. LOUIS

Copyright © 1988 Vedanta Society of St. Louis

Library of Congress Cataloging-in-Publication Data
Brahmananda, Swami, 1863-1922.
  [Dharma-prasange Swami Brahmananda. English]
  A guide to spiritual life: spiritual teachings of Swami
Brahmananda / translated with a biographical introduction by Swami
Chetanananda.—1st ed.
    p.   cm.
  Translation of: Dharma-prasange Swami Brahmananda.
  Bibliography: p.
  ISBN 0-916356-60-4
  1. Spiritual life (Hinduism)   2. Ramakrishna Mission.
3. Brahmananda, Swami, 1863-1922.   4. Hindus—India—Biography.
I. Chetanananda, Swami.   II. Title.
BL1231.32.B7313 1988   87-34048
294.5 ' 448—dc19

All rights reserved. No part of this book may be used or reproduced in any manner whatsoever without written permission, except in the case of brief quotations embodied in critical articles or reviews.

Printed in the United States of America

2 3 4 5 6 7 8 9

Those who wish to learn in greater detail about the teachings in this book may write to the Secretary, Vedanta Society of St. Louis, 205 South Skinker Boulevard, St. Louis, Missouri 63105, U.S.A.

TRANSLATOR'S PREFACE

When I first joined the monastery of the Ramakrishna Order, I used to ask spiritual questions of senior monks who were disciples of Holy Mother, Swami Vivekananda, Swami Brahmananda, or Swami Shivananda. On one occasion a monastic disciple of Swami Brahmananda told me: "Read *Dharma-prasange Swami Brahmananda* (Spiritual Teachings of Swami Brahmananda); then you will not have to ask spiritual questions of anybody." Truly speaking, that book became my spiritual guide, and I still get inspiration from it. For that reason I have translated this present book, *A Guide To Spiritual Life: Spiritual Teachings of Swami Brahmananda*, from the original Bengali, as recorded by his disciples.

Readers will feel that these teachings have come straight from the heart of Swami Brahmananda, the spiritual son of Sri Ramakrishna. The swami was a spiritual dynamo and he taught with authority. Wherever he went he created such a holy atmosphere that people around him found themselves living in a higher realm without practicing any disciplines. Swami Vivekananda once commented, "In spirituality, Brahmananda has even surpassed me."

Nowadays in the West there are so many teachers giving instructions according to their own understanding and knowledge that people often get confused by contradictory views. Thus, they go from one teacher to another, trying to fulfill their spiritual hunger. Shankara, the great philosopher of Vedanta, mentioned some signs of a true teacher: "A teacher is one who is deeply versed in the scriptures, pure, free from desires, a perfect knower of Brahman. He is firmly established in Brahman, calm like the fire when its fuel is consumed, an ocean of love without any ulterior motive, a friend to those who humbly entrust themselves to him." An aspirant must be careful in selecting a teacher. Otherwise he will suffer like a patient who has been treated by a quack doctor.

Once somebody asked Swami Brahmananda, "Is a guru necessary in spiritual life?" His answer was: "If you want to be a pickpocket, you must go to an expert pickpocket for training. You have come to realize God, so don't you need a teacher?"

I am thankful to the President of Udbodhan Office, Calcutta, for giving me permission to translate *Dharma-prasange Swami Brahmananda* into English. Some teachings in this book appeared in *Spiritual Talks,* by the First Disciples of Sri Ramakrishna, and I would like to acknowledge the help that translation provided. For further information, readers are referred to Swami Prabhavananda's *The Eternal Companion,* which includes Swami Brahmananda's life, some of his teachings, and reminiscences by his disciples and devotees.

I am grateful to the Vedanta students who helped edit and type the manuscript.

Because human beings differ from person to person, the teachers of Vedanta teach individually. The teachings for the monastics and the teachings for the householders cannot be the same, though both are pursuing the spiritual path. So I remind the readers to practice those teachings which are appealing, suitable, and beneficial to them and not to follow every teaching indiscriminately.

Readers will find the pure spiritual tradition of Vedanta in this book. It will help them to build their inner lives, to breathe the freshness of the eternal, and to attain peace, bliss, and freedom.

Vedanta Society of St. Louis Chetanananda
Golden Jubilee (1938–1988)

CONTENTS

	Page
Translator's Preface	5
Biographical Introduction by Swami Chetanananda	13

Chapters

1. Sri Ramakrishna's Outlook - Love - Training - Spiritual Instructions — 33

2. Sri Ramakrishna's Experiences and Samadhi - Ramlala - Powers — 35

3. Sri Ramakrishna's Way of Instructing - Visions and Reactions - The Master's Samadhi - Longing - Swami Vivekananda — 37

4. Holy Places - The Goal of Human Life - Swami Vivekananda - The Need of a Routine - Obstacles — 39

5. Happiness - Give up the Toys of this World - Enjoy Mangoes - Faith - Dive Deep - Be Up and Doing - Curb Desires — 42

6. Control of the Mind - Meditation - Food - The Kundalini - Initiation — 45

7. Depression - Sri Ramakrishna - Mantram, Guru, Disciple - Patience — 49

8. Time Factor in Spiritual Life - Sri Ramakrishna's Power - Sin — 51

9	Holy Company - Renunciation - How to Conquer Lust - The Need for Spiritual Disciplines - Samadhi - Unselfish Action	52
10	Show of Emotion - Steadfast Devotion - Perseverance	55
11	Sri Ramakrishna's Truthfulness and Powers of Perception - A Monk's Ego	56
12	Ram Datta's View of Sri Ramakrishna - Ramlal - Swami Ramakrishnananda - Sri Ramakrishna's Merriment and Powers	57
13	Longing - Peace - Love - Renunciation - The Guru - Pranayama - The Real and the Unreal - Existence of God - Obstacles - Holy Company and Solitude	60
14	Japam and Meditation - The Guru - Holy Company - Routine - Morality	64
15	Self-Surrender - Be Sincere - Faith in the Guru - Grace - Hold to the Truth - God is Infinite - Knowledge - Know God Alone	66
16	Character-Building - The Parlor of God - Purity - Book Learning and Spiritual Life - Money - Renunciation - Three Rare Treasures - Faith - Grace - Perseverance	70
17	God is the Wish-Fulfilling Tree - Discrimination and Renunciation - Pray to God with Heart and Soul - Self-Effort and Divine Grace	74
18	Restlessness of the Mind - Meditation - Does Sri Ramakrishna Exist?	77

CONTENTS

19	Sri Ramakrishna - Remembrance of God	79
20	Self-Control - God Is - Meditation - Earnestness - Longing	80
21	Free Will - Willpower - Comprehending the Infinite	83
22	Relief Work - Brahmacharya - Study - Work and Worship - Selfless Action	86
23	Regularity in Spiritual Life - The Play of Maya - Control of the Mind - Do or Die	89
24	Private Instructions - Faith - Brahmacharya - Control of the Tongue - Keeping Spiritual Practices a Secret - Sleep	91
25	Keep Your Experiences Private - The Spiritual Guide - How to Conquer Fear of Death - Have Faith in Yourself - Sin	94
26	Time for Meditation - The Nerve-Current - How to Control the Mind - Nonattachment - Struggle - Recollectedness - The Mystery of God	96
27	How to Control the Mind - Meditation - The Chosen Deity and the Mantram - Japam	98
28	Japam - Meditation - The Power of the Mantram - How to Control the Mind	99
29	Meditation - Auspicious Days for Japam - Moral Teachings - Meditation on the Guru	101
30	The Play of Maya - Meditation on the Formless God	102
31	The Nature of a Holy Person	103

32	Repeat the Name of the Lord - Prayer - Grace - Yearning - The Worldly Way - Surrender	104
33	Surrender - The Guru - Grace - Control of the Mind - Renunciation - Faith	109
34	The Holy City of Varanasi - Water of the Holy Ganga - The Kundalini	112
35	Japam and Purashcharana - Food - Methodical Disciplines - Meditation	113
36	Meditation - Vision - Brahmacharya - Obstacles - Grace - Hallucination vs. Vision - The Value of Rituals	116
37	Worship - Meditation - Samadhi - The Guru - Bliss - The Absolute and the Manifestation (the Nitya and the Lila)	118
38	The Kundalini - Meditation - Concentration - The Grace of the Guru	122
39	How to Acquire Taste for Spiritual Life - Struggle - Austerity - Faith - Self-Effort - Self-Surrender	123
40	Work and Worship - Brahmacharya - The Secret of Work - How to Control the Senses	126
41	The Advantage of Youth - Training the Mind - Where is Bliss? - Happiness and Misery - The Goal of Human Life	130
42	Religion in Old Age - Grace - Follow One Path - Demand from God His Vision - The Razor's Edge - Brahmacharya	133

43	Forbearance - Truth and a Harsh Truth - Power of Adjustment - Dreams - Sri Ramakrishna's Rebirth	136
44	Fix the Mind on God - Doubt and Faith - God is Beyond the Mind - Samadhi - The Three Gunas - How to Live in the World - How to Overcome Depression - Four Kinds of Worship - How to Conquer Bad Thoughts - Determine Your Ideal - The Validity of the Scriptures - About Food - Nonviolence	137
45	Austerity - Truthfulness - Lust - Desire	144
46	On the Divine Name	146
47	On Sadhana	147
48	Work is Worship	149
49	On Sri Ramakrishna and Swami Vivekananda	151
50	Miscellaneous Teachings	153
51	A Letter to a Disciple	159
	Appendix: The Guru	167
	Glossary	177
	Suggestions for Further Reading	192

Sri Ramakrishna (1836–1886)

SWAMI BRAHMANANDA
(A Biographical Introduction)

What a person thinks of day and night comes out through his lips. It is really painful for a spiritual person who thinks constantly of God to talk or hear about mundane things. Sri Ramakrishna would feel a burning sensation in his lips whenever he had to talk with worldly people. Some time before Swami Brahmananda's first visit to Dakshineswar, Sri Ramakrishna prayed to the Divine Mother: "Mother, I want someone like myself to be my constant companion. Bring me a boy who is pure-hearted and intensely devoted to you." A few days later he had a vision in which the Divine Mother placed a boy on his lap and told him, "This is your son." Sri Ramakrishna was startled and asked her in surprise, "What do you mean?" The Mother assured him that this would be his spiritual son, not a physical son. Later Sri Ramakrishna had another vision. He saw two boys dancing on a lotus, which was floating on the Ganga. One of the boys was Krishna and the other was the same boy whom the Mother had previously placed on his lap. That very day Sri Ramakrishna met Brahmananda and immediately recognized him as his spiritual son.

Swami Brahmananda's premonastic name was Rakhal Chandra Ghosh. He was born on January 21, 1863, at Sikra Kulingram, a village fifty miles from Calcutta. His father was a wealthy landlord. His mother died when he was young. From his childhood Rakhal was quiet by nature and deeply religious. When he was twelve he was sent to Calcutta to study at an English secondary school. There was a gymnasium in the city at which he exercised and where he met Narendra (later Swami Vivekananda). Being of the same age, they became close friends, and both joined the Sadharan Brahmo Samaj, a religious organization. When Rakhal was sixteen his father, noticing his spiritual tendencies, arranged his marriage. The boy obediently accepted the decision, but without any enthusiasm. Ironically, it was the bride's brother who took Rakhal to meet Sri Ramakrishna in 1881 and later made it possible for him to renounce the world.

After Rakhal's first meeting with the Master, he began to visit him now and then, and later he started staying at Dakshineswar. His father objected to this, but Rakhal's in-laws did not mind because they were very devoted to Sri Ramakrishna. One day Visweswari, Rakhal's wife, came with her mother to visit the Master. Sri Ramakrishna received them cordially and, having observed the bride closely, later said, "She represents an auspicious aspect of the divine Shakti and will not stand in her husband's way."

In Sri Ramkrishna Rakhal found a loving mother, and he behaved with the Master like a little boy. The Master treated Rakhal exactly as his own child, and even took him on his shoulders. On one occasion Sri Ramakrishna was so much struck with Rakhal's simplicity that he burst into tears and said: "You are so simple! Ah, who will look after you after I am gone?" From time to time Rakhal gave personal service to the Master, rubbing oil on his body or protecting him while he was in samadhi. At night he slept in the Master's room. The Master also taught him various kinds of spiritual disciplines and trained him to recognize people's inner nature.

On March 11, 1883, Rakhal's father came to Dakshineswar to see his son. Sri Ramakrishna received him cordially and praised Rakhal, saying: "Ah, what a nice character Rakhal has developed! Look at his face and every now and then you will notice his lips moving. Inwardly he repeats the name of God, and so his lips move.

"Youngsters like him belong to the class of the ever-perfect. They are born with God-consciousness. No sooner do they grow a little older than they realize the danger of coming in contact with the world. There is the parable of the homa bird in the Vedas. The bird lives high up in the sky and never descends to earth. It lays its egg in the sky, and the egg begins to fall. But the bird lives in such a high region that the egg hatches while falling. The fledgling comes out and continues to fall. But it is still so high that while falling it grows wings and its eyes open. Then the young bird perceives that it is dashing down toward the earth and will be instantly killed. The moment it sees the ground, it turns and shoots up toward its mother in the sky. Then its one goal is to reach its mother. Youngsters like Rakhal are like that bird."

Though the Master was extremely affectionate toward Rakhal, he did not hesitate to take him to task when he made a mistake. One day Rakhal ate butter from the temple *prasad* (offered food) without waiting for the Master to eat first, as was the custom. "How greedy you are," Sri Ramakrishna said. "You ought to have learned, from being here, to control yourself!" Rakhal was ashamed and never did it again. On another occasion Rakhal found a coin on the street, which he picked up and gave to a beggar. When he later mentioned it to Sri Ramakrishna, the Master again reprimanded him: "Why would a person who does not eat fish go to the fish market? If you do not need money, why did you touch it?" The Master wanted his spiritual son to be free from lust and greed, the two great obstacles in spiritual life.

Spiritual life is not always easy. It has many ups and downs. Rakhal had to pass through various ordeals and difficulties. One day he told the Master about his mind's dry and lethargic condition. Sri Ramakrishna did not say anything. After some time he saw Rakhal meditating in the *natmandir* (the hall in front of the Mother's temple). He approached him in a state of ecstasy and said: "Look, Rakhal. This is your mantram and there is your Chosen Deity." Immediately Rakhal saw the luminous form of God in front of him and was overwhelmed.

When Sri Ramakrishna was ill Rakhal served him till the end. Once at the Cossipore garden house, where the Master spent the last nine months of his life, he told Naren: "Rakhal has the keen intelligence of a king. If he chose, he could rule a kingdom." Naren understood that the Master wanted Rakhal to be the future leader of his disciples, so he told his brother disciples, "Henceforth, we shall call Rakhal our king." Sri Ramakrishna was pleased when he heard this. Later Rakhal became known in the Ramakrishna Order as "Maharaj," or Great King.

After Sri Ramakrishna passed away on August 16, 1886, his disciples established the Ramakrishna Monastery at Baranagore, Calcutta. They then took formal vows of monastic life and changed their names accordingly. Rakhal became Swami Brahmananda. His father tried to bring him home but failed. Swami Brahmananda cut off all family ties and attachments and became so absorbed in spiritual life that he almost forgot the world.

In *The Gospel of Sri Ramakrishna,* M. recorded a conversation he had with Rakhal in the Baranagore monastery:

Rakhal (*earnestly*): "M., let us practice *sadhana* [spiritual disciplines]! We have renounced home for good. When someone says, 'You have not yet realized God by renouncing home; then why all this fuss?', Narendra gives a good retort. He says, 'Because we could not attain Ram, must we live with Shyam and beget children?' Ah! Every now and then Narendra says nice things."

M.: "What you say is right. I see that you too have become restless for God."

Rakhal: "M., how can I describe the state of my mind?

Today at noontime I felt great yearning for the Narmada [a river in Central India the bank of which is favored by ascetics]. M., please practice sadhana; otherwise you will not succeed. Even Shukadeva was afraid of this world. That is why immediately after his birth he fled the world. His father asked him to wait, but he ran straight away."

M.: "Yes, the *Yogopanishad* describes how Shukadeva fled this world of maya. It also describes Vyasa's conversation with Shuka. Vyasa asked his son to practice religion in the world. But Shuka said that the one essential thing is the Lotus Feet of God. He also expressed his disgust with worldly men for getting married and living with women."

Rakhal: "Many people think that it is enough not to look at the face of a woman. But what will you gain merely by turning your eyes to the ground at the sight of a woman? Narendra put it very well last night, when he said: 'Woman exists for a man as long as he has lust. Free from lust, one sees no difference between man and woman.'"

M.: "How true it is! Children do not see the difference between man and woman."

Rakhal: "Therefore I say that we must practice spiritual discipline. How can one attain Knowledge without going beyond maya?"

In December 1889 Swami Brahmananda decided to practice intense austerities alone in the holy places of India. His brother disciples, however, insisted that Swami Subodhananda accompany him and look after him. The two swamis first went to Varanasi via Deoghar and stayed there for a month. From Varanasi they went to Omkarnath, situated on the bank of the holy river Narmada. Here Swami Brahmananda lived continuously in samadhi for six days, completely oblivious of the outside world. After Omkarnath they visited Panchavati, on the bank of the river Godavari, a holy place connected with the life of Ramachandra. They then went to Bombay, and from there to Dwaraka, on the shore of the Arabian Sea, a place associated with Sri Krishna. Swami Brahmananda was not an ordinary pilgrim. He saw the living presence of gods and goddesses in these holy places. Once he said, "Spiritual life begins after *nirvikalpa samadhi* [transcendental experience]."

In 1890 Swamis Brahmananda and Subodhananda arrived at Vrindaban, where they passed their time in intense spiritual practices. On March 29, the swami wrote a letter to Balaram Bose, a devotee of Sri Ramakrishna, describing his spiritual struggle: ". . . Who can understand the divine play of God? Man experiences happiness and misery according to his own karma. This is true of every man—whether he is learned or ignorant, good or wicked. Rare indeed is a person in this world who enjoys uninterrupted peace and bliss! Blessed is he who is free from desires, for he lives in the kingdom of peace. There is more misery than happiness in this world, and most people live in misery. If God is all-merciful then why do his children suffer so much? Only God knows the answer to this mystery, and not ordinary human beings.

"Man suffers because of his ignorance, which manifests as 'I' and 'mine.' The really happy and fortunate man is he who has given up his ego and has surrendered his life, mind, and intellect to God, and has nothing to call his own.

"The nature of the mind is to dwell on worldly objects, because it is created out of the three *gunas* which also constitute the outer world. It is only through divine grace that a man can withdraw his mind completely from the external objects and put it on God. . . .

"Presently my mental condition is not good at all. . . . I am praying to God that I may soon transcend body consciousness. Bless me that I may remain absorbed in the thought of the Master. That is the one desire of my heart."

In spite of all his spiritual experiences, it seems that Swami Brahmananda was feeling the agony of separation from the Master. He plunged into deep meditation and most of the time was in an indrawn mood. Swami Subodhananda would beg food for him, which he would sometimes eat and sometimes not. Though the two brother disciples lived together, they rarely spoke to each other.

Also living at Vrindaban at this time was Vijay Krishna Goswami, a Vaishnava saint who had known Swami Brahmananda when he was living with Sri Ramakrishna at Dakshineswar. One day Vijay asked him: "The Master gave you all that is covetable in spiritual life: vision and samadhi. Why then do you still practice so much austerity?" The swami humbly replied, "The experiences and visions I got by his grace, I am now trying to attain as my permanent possessions."

From Vrindaban Swami Brahmananda went to the Himalayan region at Hardwar, seeking greater solitude. He stayed at Kankhal, near Hardwar, for some time and met Swami Vivekananda and other brother disciples there. The whole party then traveled to Merut and lived there for a few months. Before he left for America in 1893, Swami Vivekananda left his brother disciples at Delhi to wander alone. Swami Brahmananda then went with Swami Turiyananda to many holy places in western and northern India, and later returned to Vrindaban.

As God tests the faith of mystics, so mystics also verify God's grace. One day Swami Turiyananda said to Swami Brahmananda: "Today I shall not go out to beg food. Let us see if Radha [the goddess of Vrindaban] will feed us." Both swamis passed the whole day and night in meditation, and the next morning a man brought various kinds of food for them. On another occasion, when they were practicing austerity near Lake Kusum (near Vrindaban), Swami Turiyananda only got some dry bread from begging. Offering that to Swami Brahmananda, he said: "Maharaj, the Master used to take such wonderful care of you. He would feed you with delicacies, and I am feeding you this dry, tasteless bread." Saying so, he burst into tears.

Monks sometimes follow the example of a python, which does not make any effort to get its food. They depend solely on God. In Vrindaban Swami Brahmananda took such a vow, and a devotee provided his food and other necessities. One day while he was meditating a man put a new blanket in front of him and left. After a short while a thief came and took the blanket. The swami silently observed the play of maya and smiled.

Temptation is one of the tests of spirituality. Once the Queen of Bharatpur came on a pilgrimage to Lake Kusum. She was very much impressed when she saw Swami Brahmananda's serene face, and she offered some sweets to him. When the swami opened one of the sweets, he found a gold coin inside. Immediately he put the sweet down and he and Swami Turiyananda left that place.

The swamis then went to Ayodhya, the birthplace of Ramachandra. They could not stay there very long as there was a terrible scarcity of food. One day Swami Turiyananda went to beg food and got some boiled *kachu* (an edible root). As soon as they ate it their throats started to sting and burn, and gradually their mouths and tongues swelled. Seeing Swami Brahmananda suffering, Swami Turiyananda went out to find a lime, which is an antidote for that allergy. He found a lime grove, but he could not see any fruit on the trees. He sought out the owner of the grove but was told that the fruit was out of season. Passing the grove again, he keenly searched the trees, when unexpectedly he saw a lime. With the permission of the owner he plucked the fruit and ran with it back to Swami Brahmananda. It immediately relieved his painful throat. That night Swami Brahmananda lamented, addressing Sri Ramakrishna: "Master, why did you take me from home if you could not provide a morsel of food? Tomorrow morning if I get hot *khichuri* [rice and lentils cooked together] and pickles, I shall understand that you are with me."

The next morning the swamis went to bathe in the river Saraju. A monk came there and said to Swami Brahmananda: "Swami, I understand both of you fasted yesterday. Please come to my cottage and have some prasad, which I offered to Lord Rama." The monk served hot khichuri and pickles to the swamis. They greatly enjoyed the meal. The monk then said: "Blessed I am! For the last twenty-four years I have been practicing sadhana here in order to have a vision or to hear the voice of Lord Rama. Today the Lord has blessed me." Tears came from the eyes of the monk. At Swami Brahmananda's request, the monk elaborated: "While I was sleeping last night I saw that Lord Rama touched my body with his soft hand and said: 'Get up! I am hungry. Cook khichuri and offer it to me. Tomorrow morning you will see two devotees bathing at the ghat of the Saraju River. They are fasting. Offer my prasad to them.' It is by your grace that I got the vision of Lord Rama." While returning to their cottage Swami Brahmananda related to Swami Turiyananda the mystery behind that incident.

During this period of his sadhana, Swami Brahmananda heard about Swami Vivekananda's success in America, where he had represented Hinduism at the Parliament of Religions in 1893. Swami Vivekananda was now urging his brother disciples to band together and carry on the mission of the Master. In January 1895 Swami Brahmananda created a great stir of enthusiasm among his brothers when he returned to them at the monastery, which was then located at Alambazar. Swami Vivekananda returned from America in 1897 and established the Ramakrishna Math and Mission, and he later made Swami Brahmananda the President of the Order.

Swami Brahmananda was an outstanding administrator and

organizer. Swami Vivekananda laid the foundation stone of Sri Ramakrishna's spiritual heritage, and Swami Brahmananda built the edifice upon it. As the Master had done, Swami Brahmananda always reminded the monks, "God first and then the world." "The one purpose of life is to know God," he would say. "Attain knowledge and devotion; then serve God in mankind. Work is not the end of life. Disinterested work is a means of attaining devotion. Keep at least three-fourths of your mind in God. It is enough if you give one-fourth to service."

Swami Brahmananda did not like to talk much about religion. It was very difficult to draw him into spiritual conversations. But when he did talk, his words flashed with fire, and those who heard him received lifelong inspiration. As a result of his spiritual influence and loving personality, many young men joined the Order. A disciple of Swami Brahmananda wrote in his reminiscences:

> Maharaj had the power to change the atmosphere of a place and to make it vibrate with his spirituality. In his company he could make everybody roll with laughter, and then suddenly, when he became silent, the place would be surcharged with a divine presence. Swami Turiyananda once remarked that Maharaj used to create such an atmosphere around himself that everyone present would be filled with some of his spiritual mood. Many people used to come to Maharaj for the purpose of seeking advice about their problems. But once they were near him they felt no necessity to ask for any solution. Problems solved themselves in his presence, and people would forget themselves, their egoism, temporal pleasure and pain, and be filled with intense divine bliss.

Girish Chandra Ghosh, a devotee of Sri Ramakrishna, told the following story about Swami Brahmananda's extraordinary spiritual power: "Compared to myself, Rakhal is only a young boy. I know that the Master regarded him as his spiritual son, but that is not the only reason I respect him. Once I was suffering from asthma and various kinds of ailments. As a result, my body became very weak and I lost faith in Sri Ramakrishna. With a view to getting rid of that dry spell, I engaged pandits to read the Gita and the Chandi to me. But still I had no peace of mind. Some brother disciples came to see me, and I told them about the unhappy state of my mind, but they only kept silent. Then one day Rakhal came and asked me, 'How are you?' I replied: 'Brother, I am in hell. Can you tell me the way out?' Rakhal listened to me and then burst into laughter. 'Why worry about it?' said he. 'As the waves of the ocean rise high, then go down again, and again rise, so does the mind. Don't be upset. Your present mood is due to the fact that it will lead you to a higher realm of spirituality. The wave of the mind is gathering strength.' As soon as Rakhal left my house, my doubt and dryness disappeared and I got back my faith and devotion."

There is no glory in making a good man better. Once Swami Brahmananda said to a monk, "If you can't make a bad man good, why did you become a monk?" The swami was a friend and savior of the fallen, the dejected, and the lowly. When Sri Ramakrishna was alive Girish took many actors and actresses of his theater to him for his blessings. It is to be noted that at that time actresses were not accepted by society. They were considered immoral women. One of the actresses, named Tara, wrote in her memoirs of how Swami Brahmananda's love and blessings changed her life:

> Ever since I was a little girl I worked on the stage with Girish Chandra Ghosh and heard from him about Sri Ramakrishna. There was a photograph of Sri Ramakrishna in every theater with which Girish Babu was connected, and

the actors and actresses used to bow down to the Master's photograph before they appeared on the stage. . . .

My first visit to the Belur Math took place about six years ago [1916]. I was then depressed and restless. Life seemed unbearable to me. I began to seek out places of pilgrimage. In this unhappy state of mind I finally went to Belur Math. Binodini, the finest actress of Bengal at the time, was with me. When I was seven years old she introduced me to the theater, and again it was she who introduced me to the monastery.

It was past noon when we came to the Math. Maharaj [Swami Brahmananda] had finished his lunch and was about to go to his room to rest. At that moment we arrived and prostrated before him.

Maharaj said: "Hello, Binode! Hello, Tara! So you have come! You are too late. We have already finished our lunch. You should have let us know that you were coming."

We could see how worried he was about us. He immediately ordered fruit prasad, and arrangements were made to fry *luchis* [fried bread] for us. We went first to the shrine, then had our prasad, and afterward were shown around the Math by a swami. Maharaj did not have his rest that day.

We were brought up to revere holy men. But along with respect and faith I felt much fear of them. I was impure—a fallen woman. And so when I touched the holy feet of Maharaj, I did it with great hesitancy, afraid to offend him. But his sweet words, his solicitude and love dispelled all my fear.

Maharaj asked me, "Why don't you come here often?" I replied, "I was afraid to come to the Math." Maharaj said with great earnestness: "Fear? You are coming to Sri Ramakrishna. What fear can there be? All of us are his children. Don't be afraid! Whenever you wish, come here. Daughter, the Lord does not care about externals. He sees our inmost heart. There should be no fear in approaching him."

I could not hold back my tears. My lifelong sorrow melted as the tears fell from my eyes, and I realized: Here is my refuge. Here is someone to whom I am not a sinner, I am not an outcast.

As President of the Ramakrishna Order, Swami Brahmananda traveled to various centers of the Order in order to guide the monks and devotees. He was a spiritual dynamo. Sister Devamata (Miss Laura Glenn, an American devotee) wrote in her *Days In An Indian Monastery*: "One evening while he [Swami Brahmananda] was at Madras, he went into samadhi during *arati* [vesper service]. He sat on the rug at the far end of the hall, his body motionless, his eyes closed, a smile of ecstasy playing about his lips. Swami Ramakrishnananda was the first to observe that he did not move when the service was over. Realizing what had occurred, he motioned to one of the young swamis to fan his head. . . . For half an hour no one stirred—a boy who was crossing the hall did not even draw back his foot. Perfect stillness pervaded the monastery—a radiant, pulsing stillness."

During Christmas time Swami Brahmananda asked Sister Devamata to arrange a Christmas party in Western fashion. She could not get a Christmas tree, but she bought plum cake, glacé fruits, and other items from an English shop. The boys brought green branches from the jungle and bound them to the pillars in the hall and decorated the entrance with mango leaves and garlands. A Christmas altar was set up, and bread and wine were offered as a symbol of the Christian Eucharist. Sister Devamata narrated the event:

> Swami Brahmananda asked me to read the story of Christ's birth and I chose the account of St. Luke. When I finished reading, the intense stillness in the air led me to

look toward Swami Brahmananda. His eyes were open and fixed on the altar, there was a smile on his lips, but it was evident that his consciousness had gone to a higher plane. No one moved or spoke. At the end of twenty minutes or more the look of immediate seeing returned to his eyes and he motioned to us to continue the service. Lights, incense and burning camphor were waved before the altar, the evening chant and hymn were sung, all those present bowed in silent prayer and the Christmas Service was ended.

As he was eating he remarked to me: "I have been very much blessed in coming to your house today, Sister." I answered quickly, "Swamiji, it is I who have been blessed in having you come." "You do not understand," he replied. "I have had a great blessing here this afternoon. As you were reading the Bible, Christ suddenly stood before the altar dressed in a long blue cloak. He talked to me for some time. It was a very blessed moment."

Though his mind dwelt most of the time in a higher realm, he keenly watched the activities of the monasteries. The interests of the swami were varied. He gave wise direction as to the design of a building; he made suggestions about the relief operations of the Mission; his recommendations on the methods of education were valued by the educators; and his advice regarding the principles to be followed in editing books proved to be extremely sound. Whenever he visited any center, he encouraged the monks to plant flowers and fruit trees and also to establish a dairy. The swami was very fond of flowers, and he could not bear it if anybody picked flowers unnecessarily or injured a flowering plant. Once Swami Brahmananda observed a monk picking flowers for worship and taking big ones from only one tree. He then taught the monk how to pick flowers, saying: "Please pick those flowers for worship which are hidden in the leaves. Don't make the tree ugly by collecting all the flowers you need from a particular tree. Rather, pick a few flowers from each tree. Those trees are also worshipping the Cosmic God with their flowers."

Swami Brahmananda was very fond of music, particularly devotional songs and the chanting of hymns and prayers. Every morning after meditation the monks would assemble in his room and would sing devotional songs. He also introduced *Ramnam Sankirtan* [choral singing in praise of Lord Rama] in the Order, and he himself would join in the singing.

At times the swami was very serious and a man of few words, but at other times he was full of fun and would play practical jokes on his brother disciples as well as on other monks. They all knew Maharaj's childlike nature. The natural tendency of his mind was to soar high, so in order to teach people he had to bring his mind down through various methods, such as teasing or mimicking others, playing cards, or catching fish. Swami Satprakashananda (a disciple of Swami Brahmananda) wrote the following incident in his memoirs:

> One day at the beginning of the winter season in 1917, in the drawing room of Balaram Mandir [Calcutta], Maharaj asked me to bring him pen, ink, and a piece of writing paper. When he began to dictate in English, I took down what he said. . . . The letter was addressed "To the Abbot, Belur Monastery." At the time, Swami Shivananda was in charge at the Belur Math, as respected Swami Premananda was lying ill in the small room adjoining the Balaram Mandir.
>
> The gist of the letter was: "The Christmas celebration will surely be observed at your Math. On that occasion we—a party of monks—are coming to the Math. Your hospitality is well known. Certainly at the conclusion of the

ceremony, according to the usual custom in Christmas celebrations, there will be an arrangement for the taking of drinks. We are nonvegetarians and are fond of varied courses of meat dishes. In anticipation of a sumptuous feast, we extend to you our heartfelt thanks. May your function be crowned with success in all possible ways—that is our earnest wish."

When I had written the letter, I handed it to him for his signature. But instead of putting his own name, he signed "Premananda" and told me, "Go and read the letter to Swami Premananda." Hearing the contents of the letter and finding his signature forged, Swami Premananda simply smiled and said, "Maharaj has a childlike nature." One thing has to be especially noted here—both Swamis Premananda and Shivananda were vegetarians.

Later Maharaj asked me to go to Belur Math and deliver the letter to Swami Shivananda, but cautioned me not to mention that he had sent it. After reading through the letter, Swami Shivananda looked at me and said, laughing: "Maharaj has sent this. Is that not so?" Without a word I nodded my head a little. Swami Shivananda understood, "Silence is acquiescence."

Swami Brahmananda collected some teachings of Sri Ramakrishna in Bengali, which were later translated into English and published under the title *Words of the Master*. When he was working on the manuscript of those teachings he would not allow anybody to stay in his room. Sometimes he would get up at midnight and ask his attendant to bring the manuscript to him. Once, after correcting it, he said, "The Master came and told me: 'I didn't say that. I said this.'" Swami Saradananda wrote in his introduction to that book: "The present brochure is from the pen of one who was regarded by the

Master as next to Swami Vivekananda in his capacity for realizing religious ideals. It is indeed the work of grateful love of the beloved disciple—one who, more than anyone else, lived constantly with the Master—to set the Master correctly before the public, seeing how his invaluable words are becoming roughly handled, deformed, and distorted nowadays at the hands of many."

Once Swami Brahmananda was waiting for a train in East Bengal (now Bangladesh) when a young girl came to the swami for advice and blessing. He said to her: "Daughter, the train is coming. I don't have much time, but I will give you knowledge in one sentence: Read *The Gospel of Sri Ramakrishna* regularly every day. That is enough. You will find in this book the truth of all religions."

Swami Brahmananda was an awakener and inspirer of souls, as his teachings came straight from his heart and experience. One disciple recorded a few of his teachings in a diary: "Keep recollectedness of God! While you are standing, while you are sitting, while you are walking—keep that recollectedness!

"You cannot buy God. His vision comes only through his grace. Does this mean that you should not practice spiritual disciplines? Certainly you must practice, otherwise passions will create havoc in you.

"Be content with your external conditions—yes, but never be content with your state of spiritual growth."

Once Maharaj asked a disciple, "Why did God create us?" Then he answered the question himself, "So that we can love him."

In March 1922, shortly after the birthday celebration of Sri Ramakrishna, Swami Brahmananda fell ill, first of cholera and then of diabetes. In spite of his physical discomfort and pain, he was constantly in an ecstatic mood. He blessed the monks and brahmacharins, saying: "Don't be afraid. Brahman alone is real and the world is unreal. Never forget God." Toward the end he had various kinds of visions. He felt that he was being carried away by the current of the blissful ocean of Brahman. Suddenly he exclaimed: "Ah, that inexpressible light! Ramakrishna! I am the cowherd boy of Vrindaban. Put anklets on my feet. I want to dance, holding the hand of my Krishna. Jhum - Jhum - Jhum! Krishna, Krishna, Krishna has come. Can't you see him? Oh, how beautiful! . . . My play is over now. Look! The child Krishna is caressing me. He is calling me to come away with him! I am coming. . . ." Swami Brahmananda passed away on April 10, 1922.

Sri Ramakrishna had predicted, "When Rakhal knows his real nature, he will not keep his body anymore." Swami Brahmananda acted in Sri Ramakrishna's divine drama the role of a king. He ruled with love, compassion, and spirituality. Once Boshi Sen, a young devotee, said to Swami Brahmananda, "Maharaj, you are miserly."

"Why do you say so?" asked the swami.

"Because you have the power to give the experience of God to others, but you are withholding it."

Swami Brahmananda gravely said, "Who wants God?"

SPIRITUAL TEACHINGS OF SWAMI BRAHMANANDA

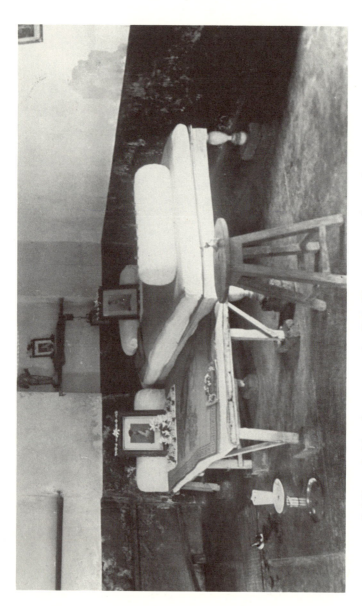

Sri Ramakrishna's room at the Dakshineswar temple garden

1

SRI RAMAKRISHNA'S OUTLOOK—LOVE—TRAINING—SPIRITUAL INSTRUCTIONS

*Place: Alambazar Monastery of the Ramakrishna
       Order of India*
Date: June 1, 1897

QUESTION: Maharaj,[1] tell us something about Sri Ramakrishna. How did he look upon people?

MAHARAJ: He looked upon all as God. Once Swami Vivekananda said to him, "Sir, since you love us so much, will you finally turn out to be another Jada Bharata?"[2] The Master [Sri Ramakrishna] replied: "One becomes a Jada Bharata by thinking about inert objects, but I think only of consciousness. The day I feel attached to you, I shall drive you all away."

One day the Master did not speak to Swamiji [Swami Vivekananda] for some reason, but Swamiji was unperturbed and remained cheerful. Observing this, the Master remarked, "He is a great soul." On another day, when Keshab Sen [a devotee of the Master] eulogized Swamiji, the Master told him: "Do not praise him so much. He has yet to blossom out."

---

[1]*Maharaj*—Literally it means "great king"; lord, master. It is an endearing title of respect used in India when addressing a man of renunciation. Swami Brahmananda is known as "Maharaj" in the Ramakrishna Order.

[2]In ancient times there was a king named Jada Bharata who spent the last years of his life as a recluse in the forest. One day he saw a pregnant deer being attacked by a lion. She jumped into the river and while trying to get back up on shore, gave birth to a fawn and died. Jada Bharata saved the fawn, raised it, and became very attached to it. At the time of his death, he was thinking of the deer and as a result was reborn as a deer. When that deer-life ended, he was again reborn as a brahmin and attained illumination. Vide: Vishnu Purana

The Master used to say: "Do you know what type of love is necessary for God-realization? As a dog with a wound in its head becomes frantic and jumps around, so one should desperately seek God."

Usually the Master would not allow anyone to stay with him for more than two or three days, but once a young man stayed with him for several days. This annoyed some devotees, and they complained to the Master that he was teaching the young man the path of renunciation. The Master answered: "Let him take up a worldly life. Am I dissuading him from it? Let him first attain knowledge and then enter the world. Do I teach everybody to renounce lust and gold? I talk about renunciation to the ones who need only a little encouragement." He used to say to the rest, "Go and enjoy the hog-plum pickle, and come here for medicine when you have colic."

Sometimes the Master would ask people: "Can you tell me what kind of state I am passing through? What makes me go so often to those who cannot buy me a penny's worth of puffed sugar cakes and who have not even the means to offer me a torn mat to sit on?" He used to explain afterward: "I find that certain people will easily attain success. It will be very difficult for the rest, for they are, as it were, pots for curd. One cannot keep milk in them." He would tell them, "I pray for you so that you may realize God quickly."

One day when the topic of the *Kartabhajas*[3] came up in the course of conversation, Girish Ghosh [a devotee of the Master] sarcastically remarked that he would write a drama about them. Hearing this, the Master gravely said: "You see, some people in that sect also have attained perfection. It too is a path."

One day Swami Turiyananda asked the Master, "How can I

---

[3]Kartabhajas—a minor sect of Vaishnavas (worshippers of Vishnu).

get rid of lust?" The Master replied: "Why should it be gotten rid of? Turn it in another direction." He said the same thing about anger, greed, infatuation, and other passions. These words of the Master inspired the young disciple.

The Master used to say, "Wherever there is extreme longing, God reveals himself more." He also said to some people: "Have love for this [pointing to himself]. That will do." Oh! Such a wonderful play is over!

2

SRI RAMAKRISHNA'S EXPERIENCES AND SAMADHI— RAMLALA—POWERS

Place: Ramakrishna Monastery, Alambazar, Calcutta
Date: July 23, 1897

Maharaj was talking about Sri Ramakrishna: It would have been wonderful if the Master's sayings, especially those about his devotional practices, spiritual unfoldment, and experiences, could have been recorded exactly and correctly—that is to say, immediately after hearing them from him. When he talked about knowledge [jnana yoga], he did not talk about anything else. Again, when he talked about devotion [bhakti yoga], he spoke of nothing but devotion. He repeatedly imprinted in our minds that worldly knowledge is insignificant and futile, that one must exert oneself to attain spiritual knowledge, devotion, and love alone.

QUESTION: Please tell us something about Sri Ramakrishna's *samadhi* [superconscious state].

MAHARAJ: The Master would go into different kinds of samadhi at different times. Sometimes his whole body would become stiff like a log. Coming down from this state, he could easily regain normal consciousness. At other times, however, when he was absorbed in deep samadhi, it would take a longer period for him to return to consciousness of the outer world. On such occasions he would take a deep breath after gasping for a while, like a drowning man coming up out of water. Even after he had composed himself, he would talk like a drunkard for some time, and not all of his speech was intelligible. At that time he would often express some small desire: "I shall eat *sukta* [a bitter squash curry]," "I shall smoke tobacco," and so on. And sometimes he would rub his face, moving his hands up and down.

Maharaj then raised a question himself and continued the conversation: Can you tell me why the Master made rapid spiritual progress without having any particular external help? It is hard to discern any cause other than a few inborn *samskaras* [tendencies]. Is it not a miracle? There are many more wonders in his life. Once a monk gave the Master a metal image of Ramlala [the child Rama]. When the Master carried that image to the Ganga for a bath, it would swim in the river. The Master himself told us this. Under such circumstances how does one differentiate between matter and consciousness?

The Master said that in the beginning he did not feel any strong desire to renounce the world, but a spiritual tempest blew over him which changed his whole life.

QUESTION: Did he possess any occult or yogic powers?

MAHARAJ: Truly I never saw any powers such as *anima* [the power to assume minute forms] or others, but he had a very clear insight into human character. I witnessed a number of supernatural things in his life.

QUESTION: Do forms like Kali, Krishna, and others really exist?

MAHARAJ: Yes, they do.

3

SRI RAMAKRISHNA'S WAY OF INSTRUCTING—VISIONS
AND REACTIONS—THE MASTER'S SAMADHI—
LONGING—SWAMI VIVEKANANDA

*Place: Belur Math, Headquarters of the Ramakrishna
Order, India*
Date: May 27, 1899

MAHARAJ: Whenever you give lectures, please use Sri Ramakrishna's teachings as much as possible because it is easy to understand the true import of the scriptures through his teachings.

The Master used to say that there should not be any theft [i.e., hypocrisy] in the inner chamber of the heart. He had great affection for the simple-hearted. He used to say: "I don't care for flattery. I love the person who calls on God sincerely." The Master also said that all impurities of the mind disappear by calling on God with a sincere heart.

Some devotees would tell the Master about their spiritual experiences. Hearing them, one young disciple[1] asked the Master to grant him some spiritual experiences. The Master told him: "Look. That kind of experience comes when one practices meditation and prayer regularly and systematically. Wait. You will get it eventually."

A couple of days later, in the evening, the young disciple saw the Master walking toward the Divine Mother's temple, and he followed him. Sri Ramakrishna entered the temple, but the disciple did not dare go inside, so he sat in the natmandir [the hall in front of the Mother's temple] and began to medi-

---

[1]This young disciple was Swami Brahmananda himself.

tate. After awhile he suddenly saw a brilliant light, like that of a million suns, rushing toward him from the shrine of the Divine Mother. He was frightened and ran to the Master's room.

A little later Sri Ramakrishna returned from the shrine. Seeing the young disciple in his room, he said: "Hello! Did you sit for meditation this evening?" "Yes, I did," answered the young disciple, and he related to the Master what had happened. Then the Master told him: "You complain that you don't experience anything. You ask, 'What is the use of practicing meditation?' So why did you run away when you had an experience?"

Usually Sri Ramakrishna never slept for more than an hour or so at night. He would pass the night sometimes in samadhi, sometimes singing devotional songs, and sometimes chanting the Lord's name. I often saw him in samadhi for an hour or more. In that state he could not talk in spite of repeated efforts. Regaining outer consciousness, he would say: "Look. When I am in samadhi I want to tell you my experiences, but at that time I lose my power of speech." After samadhi, he used to mutter something. It seemed to me that he was talking with somebody. I heard that in earlier years the Master stayed in samadhi most of the time.

Sri Ramakrishna used to say, "One needs intense longing to realize God." In this connection, the Master often told this story: Once an aspirant asked his teacher how to realize God. The teacher, without answering, took the disciple to the nearest pond and held him under the water. After awhile, when the student was extremely restless and about to collapse, the teacher pulled him out of the water and asked, "How did you feel under the water?" "I was dying for a breath of air," he answered. "When you feel like that for God," said the teacher, "you will realize him."

At first Swami Vivekananda [then known as Narendra] indulged in a lot of dry discussion with the Master. At that time he believed that God was only formless. He even told the Master, "Sir, these visions of yours are all hallucinations." He used to ridicule those who bowed down to the gods and goddesses in the temples. Some devotees were annoyed with Swamiji for this, but the Master was never irritated with him. The Master said, "Nowadays it is hard to find a soul like Naren." Later, when the Master showed Swamiji forms of gods and goddesses, he began to believe in them. From then on Swamiji would say, "If one has steadfast devotion for God, whether with form or without form, one attains perfection."

4

HOLY PLACES—THE GOAL OF HUMAN LIFE—SWAMI VIVEKANANDA—THE NEED OF A ROUTINE—OBSTACLES

Place: Ramakrishna Mission Sevashram, Kankhal (Hardwar)
Year: 1912

MAHARAJ: This place [Hardwar] is very sacred. It is not hard to attain good concentration here. The very atmosphere is pure. The holy Ganga is flowing nearby, and on the other side are the majestic Himalayas. This environment naturally induces the mind to become calm and meditative. One can hear the uninterrupted sound of OM in the wind. Having come to such a holy place, it will be really unfortunate if you spend your time in sleep and idleness. It would be much better to give up the body here practicing meditation and austerity.

Human birth is for the attainment of knowledge and devotion, and not for eating, sleeping, and begetting children like animals. God manifests himself the most in the human body. Try to realize that. Have you not heard how the disciples of Sri Ramakrishna underwent severe austerities in order to experience the truth? It was the blazing fire, the tangible spirituality, of the Master, that inspired us to practice so hard. It may not be possible for you to do as we did, but at least try.

Swami Vivekananda gave his very life to build this organization [the Ramakrishna Order] so that you could practice spiritual disciplines without much hardship. For your sake he overworked himself and died at a young age. What an encompassing love he had for all! Don't be ungrateful to him. He had great faith in the younger generation. He entrusted his mission to you. Be true and loyal to him. Sri Ramakrishna manifested himself to the world through Swami Vivekananda and gave his message through him. Know for certain that Swamiji's words and the Master's words are the same. Sri Ramakrishna was too great for the ordinary mind to understand. Swamiji presented Sri Ramakrishna and his ideals to the world in a way that ordinary people could understand. All blessed souls will have to come under his banner.

Read Swami Vivekananda's works carefully, and whenever you do not understand any point ask Shuddhananda or other swamis to explain it. Swamiji preached Sri Ramakrishna's ideals in a form intelligible to all. It is madness to try to understand Sri Ramakrishna without going through Swamiji's teachings. Study Swamiji's works and Sri Ramakrishna's teachings again and again, and plunge yourselves into meditation. If you cannot discipline your mind now, you will repent later. You are young and this is the best period of your life. Utilize it fully. Once you train your mind, you need not fear. You will then be able to turn your mind in any direction you like. As a trained horse is under the control of its master, so the mind must be brought under your control. When this is done, know that you have made significant progress. Always whip the restless mind. Scold the mind if it tries to move in the wrong direction. Never give any license to the mind.

In the beginning of spiritual life, it is very important to establish a routine with fixed hours for *japam* [repetition of a mantram], meditation, and study. Whether you like it or not, it does not matter. You must follow the routine. Have a firm resolution about it. If you continue your routine strictly for some days, a habit will be formed. Now you may not like to practice meditation, but later it will be painful to miss it. When such a state is attained, it means that you are slowly progressing toward the ideal. Know that you are nearing God when you feel as restless for his vision as a hungry and exhausted man for food and sleep.

First get a taste of Divine Nectar and become immortal. Then, come what may, whether you are cast onto the street or placed on a throne, both will seem the same to you. When iron is turned into gold by the touch of the philosopher's stone, it does not matter whether it is kept in a safe or buried in the ground. The Master used to say, "Place the knowledge of Advaita [Nondual Brahman] in your pocket, and then act as you please." In other words, after attaining knowledge and devotion and realizing God, whatever work you do will not bind you. There will be no more chance of taking a false step.

The spiritual path is full of obstacles. The Divine Mother does not easily release human beings from the bonds of her maya. To obtain her grace one should cry and pray. You have accumulated many samskaras in past lives, and you are acquiring new ones in this present life. All through your life you will have to fight against those samskaras. The more you resist them, the more they will strike back. Never yield to them or deviate from your goal. March on! You will win.

There are two tendencies in human nature—good and bad.

They are always at war. The former pushes a person toward renunciation and the latter pushes a person toward worldly enjoyment. The victory of the one over the other determines a person's nature.

Seeing innumerable objects of enjoyment in this world, people become so attached to them that they forget there is another side to the picture. They think: "No one can be sure of the future. Why shouldn't we enjoy what we have now? No one knows whether God can be realized or not, whether eternal bliss can be attained or not. But to enjoy the world is within our reach. Therefore, why should we give it up?" Consequently, they rush headlong toward sense enjoyments. But when they experience pain and misery from worldly pleasures, they realize they have made a mistake. Then they seek peace. But it is too late to attain peace. Their overindulgent lives have made them slaves to their passions. They are helpless even though they want to change their way of life.

5

HAPPINESS—GIVE UP THE TOYS OF THIS WORLD— ENJOY MANGOES—FAITH—DIVE DEEP—BE UP AND DOING—CURB DESIRES

Place: Ramakrishna Mission Sevashram, Kankhal, (Hardwar)
Year: 1912

MAHARAJ: Everyone wants happiness. Who wants pain and misery? But how do we attain happiness? Can anyone attain it by running after the fleeting pleasures of the world and ignoring God, who is the source of all happiness? He has created many playthings to delude human beings. Throw away all these and pray to him. He will then hasten to take you in his arms. Choose either God or his playthings. You can't have both.

You have had much play in your life. It is now time to give it up and call on the Divine Mother. A mother provides toys for the child who is fond of playing, but she picks up the child who does not care for toys or playing. The child who sits on the mother's lap is happy. Moreover, toys create various problems. A child feels bad when a toy falls from his hand and breaks. Again, he feels bad if he gets beaten while fighting over a toy with a playmate. But the child in the mother's lap has no such troubles. He knows the mother will supply all his needs.

The Master used to tell the story of the mango grove, saying: "You have come here to eat mangoes. Why do you bother yourself by calculating the number of trees, branches, and leaves? Eat the mangoes and be satisfied." You have come to this world for God-realization. Accomplish this first. Solve your own problems and equip yourself for life's journey. Ask yourself, "Why have I come to this world?" Struggle hard. Jump into the ocean of Satchidananda[1] and be immortal. Pray to the Lord day and night. In whatever way you call on or think of him, it will certainly do you good. You will get his vision.

Once Parvati asked Shiva, "Lord, how can one experience Satchidananda?" "Through faith," answered Shiva. You have been shown the right path. Now follow it with faith. Be up and doing. Assimilate these precious teachings into your life. Waste no more time in discussing the forms and details of your *sadhana* [spiritual practice]. In whatever way you call on

---

[1] Absolute Existence, Absolute Consciousness, and Absolute Bliss. This term is used to describe Brahman, the Ultimate Reality.

him, you will get the result. The Master used to say: "One may eat a cake with icing either straight or sideways. It will taste sweet either way." You are all seated under the *kalpataru* [the wish-fulfilling tree], and you will get whatever you ask for.

Do not think yourselves too clever. The crow thinks that it is very clever, but it lives on filth. Those who try to be very shrewd in this world are cheated in the long run.

Dive deep into the ocean of Satchidananda with faith, and you will surely reach him. Don't be discouraged if after a little practice you do not realize God. The ocean is full of precious pearls. If you don't get them in one dive, that does not mean the ocean is without pearls.

The Master used to say: "There is a kind of oyster that constantly floats about on the surface of the sea with its shell wide open. But when it catches a raindrop while the star Svati is in the ascendant, it dives down to the bottom of the sea and does not come up again." Similarly, you have received the precious mantram from your guru. Now dive deep into the sea of devotion without looking further at worldly things.

Practice your sadhana with patience and perseverance. Positively, God's grace will dawn on you in due time. As one has to follow certain protocol and satisfy the guards in order to visit a wealthy man, so one has to undergo many spiritual practices and keep the company of the holy in order to have God-realization. Know for certain that God is your very own. Pray to him for his vision. Cry to him for his grace like a little child. Can the mother stay away after hearing the cry of her child? So it is with the Lord. He reveals himself to that devotee who has longing.

Exert yourself wholeheartedly for God-realization. Make the mind one-pointed like the mariner's compass. In whatever direction the ship sails, the compass always points to the north, keeping the ship on its course. Similarly, if a man's mind is fixed on God, he has nothing to fear. He never loses his faith and devotion even when surrounded by worldly people. The moment he hears any talk about God, he becomes intoxicated with devotion and love. Do you know what he is like? He is like a flint which may remain under water for a hundred years but will still ignite as soon as it is struck. He who has realized God cannot put his mind on worldly affairs anymore. He remains absorbed in divine bliss. He does not care for anything in this world except spiritual talk and holy company. He lives in the world like a cast-off leaf in a gale, blown according to the direction of the wind. He does not have any desire of his own or any ego. Such a person can live in the world as well as in the realm of Satchidananda.

Your minds are still simple, pure, and devoid of worldly desires. Try to make this state of mind permanent. Once the mind is stained it is almost impossible to clean it. The spotless mind is like a dry match stick: it ignites the moment it is struck. But if it is wet, it won't light though you strike it a thousand times. It is extremely difficult to erase bad impressions from the mind.

6

CONTROL OF THE MIND—MEDITATION—FOOD—THE KUNDALINI—INITIATION

Place: Belur Math
Date: April 25, 1913

QUESTION: How can I control the restless mind?

MAHARAJ: Practice japam and mediation regularly. Don't miss a single day. The mind is like a restless boy. It continually runs around. You must bring the mind under control again and again and engage it in meditation on the Chosen Deity. If you continue this struggle for two or three years, the mind will gradually be calm and you will feel an unspeakable bliss in your heart. In the beginning japam and meditation seem dry, but you must engage the mind forcibly in contemplation of the Chosen Deity. It is like swallowing a bitter medicine to get rid of fever. Slowly spiritual joy will flow within you. People work so hard to pass examinations, but God-realization is far easier. One should call on God sincerely with a serene mind.

QUESTION: Maharaj, your words fill me with hope, but sometimes I feel very much depressed. I think all my spiritual disciplines are in vain since I have not had any realization.

MAHARAJ: No, no, there is no reason to be depressed. Work must have its effect. If you repeat the Lord's name either wholeheartedly or halfheartedly, it must produce results. Practice spiritual instructions systematically for some time. You will get peace and joy. Meditation gives not only mental peace but also physical health, and you will not suffer as much illness. So one should practice meditation even for good health.

In the initial stage meditation is like holding regular warfare with the mind. Steady the vacillating mind and fix it on the Chosen Deity. After awhile the brain will get a little heated. For this reason, in the beginning one should not exert the brain by overdoing spiritual disciplines. Slowly increase the time you spend in disciplines. Practicing in this way for some time, you will get real meditation. Then you will not feel any discomfort even if you sit for two to four hours. Rather, you will feel as refreshed and joyful as you feel after a sound sleep.

In the beginning of spiritual life it is extremely important to watch one's diet. The body and the mind have a close relationship. If the body becomes sick due to poor diet, meditation is impossible. Because of this there are so many rules and restrictions for an aspirant about diet. One is supposed to eat food that is easily digestible, nutritious, and not stimulating. Overeating increases *tamoguna* [inertia]. Fill half of the stomach with food and one quarter with water, leaving one quarter empty for air movement.

Is meditation an easy thing? The day you eat a little too much you cannot concentrate. Meditation is possible only when one can subdue the unseen enemies like lust, anger, greed, infatuation, and so on. Spiritual life demands austerity. It is easy to sit surrounded by fire[1] as an austerity, but the real austerity is to control the onslaught of lust and anger.

Without meditation the mind cannot be calm, and again, without calmness of the mind, meditation is not possible. If you think that when the mind is calm you will practice meditation, you will never get a chance for meditation. You must strive for both simultaneously. The desires of the mind appear and disappear like bubbles. During meditation, think of them as unreal. The more you eradicate your bad tendencies, the more your good tendencies will fill the mind. During meditation some see light, some hear the sound of OM or a bell or a distant resonance. These are not real experiences. One should move forward. But these signs are good. They indicate that one is on the right track.

A man was very wise. Fifteen days before his death he said to his family: "Please take me to the bank of the holy river Ganga. Do you think I want to die at home?" Just before his death, when his body was carried to the Ganga, he addressed

---

[1] A spiritual austerity called *Panchatapa* (lit., five fires). Four fires are set in four corners, a certain distance apart—or sometimes a complete circle of fire is made. The aspirant sits in the center, from sunrise to sunset, meditating or repeating a mantram, with the sun (the fifth fire) above.

the Divine Mother, saying: "Mother, I know of your purifying power, and I committed so many sins. Now please wash away all my impurities." Saying so, he passed away. God-realization is possible when one has such faith and devotion.

Swami Vivekananda used to say: "Only a little rousing of the *kundalini* [spiritual energy] is very dangerous. If the kundalini moves among the lower *chakras* [centers of consciousness], without rising to the higher ones, a person experiences tremendous lust and anger. So, except for advanced souls, the sweet and intimate relationship with God of the Vaishnava tradition is extremely dangerous. Beginners are not advised to read the stories of the *raslila* [the episode of Krishna's play with the gopis]."

QUESTION: Maharaj, is initiation really necessary? Can't one practice wholeheartedly according to one's spiritual mood?

MAHARAJ: Without initiation one cannot have concentration, because the mind changes and fluctuates. Today it may like the form of Kali, tomorrow Hari, the next day perhaps the formless aspect of God. Thus the mind is never concentrated upon any one ideal. Without concentration one cannot perform worldly duties properly, what to speak of God-realization!

To realize God one needs a guru. The guru selects the mantram and the Chosen Deity according to the nature of the disciple. The disciple must have faith in the words of his guru and follow his instructions with steadfast devotion; otherwise he won't make any progress. The path of spirituality is extremely difficult. A person may be intelligent and may strive hard, but without the guidance of a perfect guru, that person will definitely stumble in the spiritual path. Even to become a thief one needs a teacher, so don't you need a guru to attain the highest knowledge of Brahman?

If you want to realize God, practice spiritual disciplines with patience. Time is a vital factor. Only God knows when he will reveal himself to you. Don't be impatient. The Master used to say, "The bird hatches her egg at the right time." This period of spiritual life is extremely painful. Hope and hopelessness, laughter and tears—they alternate day after day until God is realized. But a real guru can lift the mind of the disciple quickly from that state. This act of the guru, however, may injure the growth of the disciple if the disciple is not able to withstand the onrush of this spiritual force. So the guru waits for the right time. In this state one must move cautiously. Follow the instructions of your guru implicitly. Eat *sattvic* [simple and nutritious] food and practice self-control. Otherwise you may suffer from dizziness or various kinds of ailments.

7

DEPRESSION—SRI RAMAKRISHNA—MANTRAM, GURU, DISCIPLE—PATIENCE

Place: Belur Math
Date: April 30, 1913

QUESTION: Maharaj, I was instructed to practice japam and meditation simultaneously, but I cannot meditate at all, and this often makes me extremely dejected.

MAHARAJ: It is natural to experience depression now and then. I also felt like that once while I was in Dakshineswar. I was then quite young and the Master was about fifty years old, so I was shy about speaking openly with him. One day I was meditating in the Kali temple. I could not concentrate my mind. This made me very sad. I said to myself: "I have been living here so long, yet I have not achieved anything. What is the use of staying here then? Forget it! I am not going to say anything about it to the Master. If this depressed condition continues another two or three days, I shall return home. There my mind will be occupied with different things." Having decided this in the shrine, I returned to the Master's room. The Master was then walking on the verandah. Seeing me, he also entered the room. It was customary after returning from the shrine to salute the Master and then eat a light breakfast. As soon as I saluted the Master, he said, "Look. When you returned from the shrine, I saw that your mind seemed to be covered with a thick net." I realized that he knew everything, so I said, "Sir, you know the bad condition of my mind." He then wrote something on my tongue. Immediately I forgot all my painful depression and was overwhelmed with an inexpressible joy.

As long as I lived with him I had spontaneous recollection and contemplation of God. An ecstatic joy filled me all the time. That is why one requires a powerful guru—one who has realized God. Before initiation the guru and the disciple should test each other for a long time. Otherwise there may be regrets afterward. This is no passing relationship.

When a person asks me for a mantram, I first send him away. If he persists, I give him a holy name and ask him to repeat that name one thousand times every day for one year. This turns away many people.

There is much work involved in initiating a disciple. I have to meditate long hours to select the Chosen Deity of each disciple. One day a man came to me for initiation. I thought that if I could know his Chosen Deity in meditation, I would initiate him, otherwise not. After one hour's meditation, I saw the form of a Deity and later came to know from him that that was his favorite Deity. Nowadays most people do not do anything after initiation. It is not wise to initiate one and all indiscriminately.

Immense patience is necessary in spiritual life. Go on practicing hard until you realize God. At first spiritual practice seems to be drudgery, like learning the alphabet. Then gradually peace comes. When a person complains after initiation, "Maharaj, I am not attaining anything," I do not listen to him for a couple of years. Later he himself acknowledges that he is making progress. It is not a matter for impatience. Practice your spiritual disciplines sincerely for two or three years; then you will get bliss.

8

TIME FACTOR IN SPIRITUAL LIFE—SRI RAMAKRISHNA'S POWER—SIN

Place: Belur Math
Date: May 4, 1913

Swami Brahmananda was speaking with several monks and devotees. K., a lawyer, had just asked the swami several questions relating to his spiritual practice.

MAHARAJ: It is no use hurrying oneself. Until the right time comes, it is of little avail. The condition of the mind before the favorable time arrives is really painful. The mind is swept alternately by hope and despair, smiles and tears. But if you have a proficient spiritual guide, he may, by means of spiritual processes, push your mind above this level. You may not, however, be able to stand it if you are pushed up too quickly and too high. For example, take the case of Mathur Babu, who attained *bhava samadhi* [ecstasy] by the grace of the Master but could not bear it. At last he begged the Master to take it back.

Oh, what superhuman power the Master had! At that time we thought it was merely a peculiar power with him, but we could not understand the nature of it. Now we realize what a wonderful power it was! One day I said to him: "Sir, I cannot get rid of lust. What shall I do?" He touched me in the region of the heart, muttering some indistinct words. All lust vanished from me forever! I have never felt its existence since then. Do you see the wonder of it?

Do not disturb the mind by thinking of sins, for however great a sin may be, it is great only in the eyes of men and not of God. His one glance can erase the sins of millions of births. But of course there is the effect of karma. If you do any wrong action, you must suffer from disquiet of the mind and other consequences.

9

HOLY COMPANY—RENUNCIATION—HOW TO CONQUER LUST—THE NEED FOR SPIRITUAL DISCIPLINES—SAMADHI—UNSELFISH ACTION

Place: Belur Math
Date: May 10, 1913

After the morning meditation Swami Brahmananda was in his room. Some monks and devotees sat in front of him on the floor.

MAHARAJ: Ask me whatever you wish to know.
DEVOTEE: Maharaj, how can one be devoted to God?
MAHARAJ: By association with the holy. But merely visiting the monks is not sufficient. You must build your character by

observing their lives and trying to follow their teachings. One cannot assimilate their holy nature and spiritual instructions without practicing *brahmacharya* [continence] and meditation. Similarly, by merely reading the scriptures one cannot grasp their true meaning. Regularly read *The Gospel of Sri Ramakrishna* and similar books and try to understand their meaning. The more you read, the more new ideas will flash in your mind. An aspirant understands God in one way by hearing, in another way by practicing spiritual disciplines, and in still another way by realizing him.

If you want to realize God or see him, you will have to sincerely practice spiritual disciplines. You will have to call on him with a longing heart and give up everything for him. As long as you have any desire for lust and gold or name and fame, there is no chance for God-realization. Nag Mahashay [a great devotee of Sri Ramakrishna] used to say: "What is the use of rowing the boat if it is anchored? Name and fame are easy to attain but extremely difficult to give up. He who can renounce them is a true holy man."

DEVOTEE: How can a person conquer lust?

MAHARAJ: By repeating the name of God and by contemplation on him. Do you understand?

DEVOTEE: But I cannot conquer it in any way.

MAHARAJ: Then marry. Always reason. Other people accomplish many things. Why shouldn't you? You must. Call on God in whatever way you like—meditate on him, repeat his name, or sing his praise. Do not doubt. Do not lose self-confidence.

*   *   *

Vain is your life if, having this precious human life, you do not try to realize God. Shankara said, "It is through God's grace that a person obtains these three rare things—human birth, longing for liberation, and association with a great soul."

DEVOTEE: Maharaj, some people believe that it is enough to visit holy men, and that one need not practice any other disciplines.

MAHARAJ: Don't listen to them. Simply visiting the holy men is not enough. If you have questions, ask them and remove your doubts. Observe their lives closely and follow what they say. It is self-deception if one thinks that visiting a holy man is enough and that disciplines are not necessary. On the other hand, holy company is necessary. Seeing and hearing holy people, spiritual feelings arise in the mind and doubts go away. One imbibes deeper impressions by observing a pure, God-intoxicated life than by reading hundreds of books. Adhar Sen [a devotee of Sri Ramakrishna] used to visit the Master quite often accompanied by a school subinspector, who sometimes experienced ecstasy. One day when they arrived at Dakshineswar the Master was in samadhi. There was such a smile on his face, as if it could not contain so much joy. Then Adhar said to his friend: "Seeing your trance, I conceived a disgust for it. It seemed to suggest great suffering within you. Can divine ecstasy ever cause pain? The blissful ecstasy of the Master has opened my eyes. I would have found it impossible to come here anymore if his ecstasy had been like yours." Doubt would have remained in Adhar's mind had he not gone to the Master and seen his samadhi. This is the result of holy company. If you want to realize the truth, you will have to work hard. There is no other way. Do you understand?

DEVOTEE: Maharaj, how should we live in this world? Shouldn't we practice desirelessness?

MAHARAJ: Desirelessness, unselfish action, and so on are lofty words. It is almost impossible to practice desirelessness in family life. A person may think he is working without motive, but if he analyzes carefully he will notice that there must be some kind of desire behind his actions. Do your duty in this world and pray, "Lord, reduce my activities so that I can call on you more."

10

SHOW OF EMOTION—STEADFAST DEVOTION—PERSEVERANCE

Place: Belur Math
Date: May 19, 1913

QUESTION: Maharaj, the other day you said that there is no use in hurrying oneself—that one must wait for the proper time. Should we then give up yearning for the Lord?

MAHARAJ: I might have said that in another connection. What I meant by "hurrying oneself" was displaying temporary emotional outbursts such as crying and other outward manifestations. Such fits pass in a few days. Then the person succumbs to despair and depression and gives up all search for God.

It is not good to express one's spiritual feelings. It reduces the intensity of one's longing. Once Radhaballabh Goswami, a disciple of Rupa Goswami, danced in ecstasy while performing the worship. Rupa asked the disciple to leave because he was not serving the Lord properly due to his own personal joy. Then Radha requested Rupa through a dream to take back that disciple. But Rupa told her: "You are a daughter of a milkman. What do you know about spiritual disciplines? By the grace of my guru [Chaitanya] I know how to discipline a disciple." He was such an uncompromising saint that he would not accept even Radha's suggestion. Imitating Chaitanya's ecstasy, some people exhibit exuberant emotion. For the last twelve years of his life, Chaitanya was almost constantly in a God-intoxicated state. An ordinary human being could not bear an iota of his joy or pang of separation from the Lord.

QUESTION: Sri Ramakrishna used to say that if a person goes on digging for a well at different places, he never gets any water. Is this true in spiritual life also?

MAHARAJ: Yes, it is so. One must persevere. If restlessness comes from real love for God, then one may not see him but one cannot forget him. Even if a person does not see God for millions of lives, still he will steadily call on him. Most people cannot call on God wholeheartedly because they have the idea of "give and take." Therefore, after a few calls, if they do not get any response from God, they lose hope.

11

SRI RAMAKRISHNA'S TRUTHFULNESS AND POWERS OF PERCEPTION—A MONK'S EGO

Place: Belur Math
Date: May 27, 1913

Swami Brahmananda was reminiscing about Sri Ramakrishna to the monks.

MAHARAJ: Oh, how deep was the Master's devotion to truth! If he happened to say that he would not eat any more food, he could not eat more, even if he was hungry. Once he said that he would go to visit Jadu Mallick [whose garden house was adjacent to the Dakshineswar temple garden] but later forgot all about it. I also did not remind him. After supper he suddenly remembered the appointment. It was quite late at night, but he had to go. I accompanied him with a lantern in my hand. When we reached the house we found it closed and all apparently asleep. The Master pushed back the doors of the living room a little, placed his foot inside the room, and then left.

He could see the inside of a man by merely looking at his face, as though he were looking through a glass pane. Whenever a visitor came he would look him over from head to foot, and he would understand everything. Then he would answer that person's questions.

Even great saints cannot always give up egotism. Swami Bhaskarananda [of Varanasi] showed me his own photograph and said, "See, my picture is being sold!" But the Master! When Keshab Sen wrote about him in his paper, the Master forbade him to do so again.

One day the son of a public woman came to Dakshineswar. The Master was sleeping in his room. The man entered and touched his feet. The Master at once jumped up, as if someone had thrown fire on him. He said: "Tell me frankly all the sins you have committed. If you cannot, then go to the Ganga and say them loudly. You will be freed from them." But the man was ill-fated and could not do so.

12

RAM DATTA'S VIEW OF SRI RAMAKRISHNA—RAMLAL—
SWAMI RAMAKRISHNANANDA—SRI RAMAKRISHNA'S
MERRIMENT AND POWERS

Place: Belur Math
Date: May 28, 1913

QUESTION: Maharaj, some believe that whoever has seen Sri Ramakrishna is saved. Ram Datta [a devotee of the Master] also held that view.

MAHARAJ: Ram Datta's case was exceptional. He had genuine faith in the Master. Toward the end of his life he renounced everything in pursuit of God. Others profess verbally without having true faith.

QUESTION: Maharaj, some believe that since they have seen Holy Mother [the spiritual consort of Sri Ramakrishna] and are serving the holy men, they don't need to practice any spiritual disciplines.

MAHARAJ: It is not enough merely to see Holy Mother and to serve the monks. One must practice concentration and meditation, dispassion and discrimination.

*   *   *

At night Swami Brahmananda, Ramlal (a nephew of the Master), and a few devotees were in the upper verandah of the main building of Belur Math.

RAMLAL: The other day T. of Belgharia [a devotee of the Master] came to Dakshineswar. He is now employed at Sealdah. He has married for the second time and has many children. He seems to be very entangled. He has lost his former beautiful appearance.

MAHARAJ: What a pure mind he had in those days! Even now he has it. The Master selected his men with great care. N. possessed such a high spiritual state! But the Master said, "If that is really so, why doesn't his cloth slide off his waist?" When he learned that N. had ten thousand rupees deposited in a bank, he remarked: "That is why it is so. He who is calculating is lost."

While returning to his home, Ramlal asked Swami Brahmananda a few questions.

RAMLAL: Maharaj, shall I go to Kamarpukur [the native village of Sri Ramakrishna and Ramlal] or should I send Shibu [another nephew of the Master] there? What do you suggest?

MAHARAJ: Brother, I don't know. Ask somebody else. Nowadays I don't have the state of mind to give advice to people. We are monks. To us "Brahman alone is real and the world is unreal." All these years I have thought of this world as unreal, so it is hard for me to give advice on unreal matters.

RAMLAL: Maharaj, to whom shall we go then? Whom shall we ask?

MAHARAJ: Brother, my mind is very disturbed [because of Swami Ramakrishnananda's passing away and Swami Turiyananda's illness]. Now I love to be alone. I don't want too many people around me anymore. I wish I could go to Varanasi and live there. Those with whom I was very intimate are passing away one by one. The last time I went to South India I stayed with Ramakrishnananda for six months. Those were wonderful days! None but Ramakrishnananda absorbed the ideal of the Master to such a great extent. He spent one thousand rupees on my pilgrimage. I protested when he arranged for my journey by first class, but inwardly I was pleased because it showed he had no attachment to money. A monk should be like that. One should not be calculating. Now I get joy living with Turiyananda, but he also is not well. Perhaps he won't live long. He is still alive because of his unbroken chastity since childhood and his good health.

*   *   *

MAHARAJ: Ah, how joyfully we lived with the Master at Dakshineswar! Sometimes by his humor and wit we would be convulsed with side-splitting laughter! What we now cannot experience by meditation, we then attained automatically. If my mind went astray even a little, he would understand it from my appearance and would pass his hand over my chest, setting my mind right. And how free I was with him! One day, on the semicircular west porch, I was rubbing oil on his body. For some reason I got angry with him. I threw away the bottle of oil and strode off with the intention of never returning. I got as far as Jadu Mallick's garden house but could not move further. I sat down. In the meantime he had sent Ramlal to call me back. When I returned he said: "Look. Could you go? I drew a boundary line there."

On another occasion I did something wrong and became extremely penitent. I went to confess it to him. As soon as I arrived he asked me to follow him with his water jug. While returning he said: "You did this certain thing yesterday. Never do it again." I was surprised. I wondered how he had known.

Another day when I returned from Calcutta he said: "Why can't I look at you? Have you done anything wrong?" "No," I replied, because I understood "wrong action" to mean stealing, robbery, adultery, and so on. The Master again asked me, "Did you tell any lie?" Then I remembered that the day before, while chatting and joking, I had told a fib.

13

LONGING—PEACE—LOVE—RENUNCIATION—THE GURU—PRANAYAMA—THE REAL AND THE UNREAL—EXISTENCE OF GOD—OBSTACLES—HOLY COMPANY AND SOLITUDE

Place: Belur Math
Date: June 1, 1913

It was a Sunday afternoon. Swami Brahmananda was seated with some devotees. One of them asked: Maharaj, how can one have yearning for the Lord?

MAHARAJ: Yearning comes when the mind becomes pure through the company of the holy and practicing spiritual disciplines according to the instructions of a guru.

DEVOTEE: How can one have peace?

MAHARAJ: By loving God and by having true faith in him. One cannot attain peace in the very beginning. One has to cry with a longing heart and be restless for the vision of God. Then slowly comes peace. When a person does not find any peace through worldly enjoyments and becomes disgusted with them, then he feels attracted to God. The more restless you are, the more you hunger for peace. The more thirsty you are, the more you crave water. If you really want peace, increase your inner restlessness for God.

DEVOTEE: How can one have love for God?

MAHARAJ: By meditation, devotional practices, prayer, and so on.

DEVOTEE: Can a person realize God while living in the world?

MAHARAJ: Does anyone live outside the world?

DEVOTEE: No, Maharaj, what I mean is this: Is it possible for a householder to realize God?

MAHARAJ: Then say that. Yes, one can, but with great difficulty.

DEVOTEE: Should one renounce the world if dispassion arises?

MAHARAJ: Yes, one should. That is called renunciation. When true dispassion dawns in the heart, it spreads more and more, like a wild forest fire. As Sri Ramakrishna used to say: "A fish gets relief and joy when it escapes from the net. It never wants to be trapped again. Similarly, when a person gets rid of the bondage of worldly life, he never wants to be caught again."

DEVOTEE: Is it possible to realize God without a guru?

MAHARAJ: It seems to me—no. It is not possible to realize God without a guru. It is the guru who points out the path of the Chosen Deity through a mantram. One may have many *upagurus,* or subsidiary teachers. The real guru instructs:

"Follow these spiritual disciplines and have the company of the holy." In ancient days it was the custom for the disciple to live in his guru's house. The guru would keep watch over his disciple, and the disciple would serve his guru. If the disciple went astray, the guru would bring him back to the right path. One should not accept a person as one's guru unless he is a knower of Brahman or a soul highly advanced in spirituality.

DEVOTEE: How can one recognize a perfect guru?

MAHARAJ: One can know if one lives with him for some time. The guru is supposed to observe the life of the disciple. If he sees that the disciple has tremendous attachment for worldly enjoyments, which can hardly be controlled, he should not initiate the disciple, but send him back to the world. And if he sees that the disciple is endowed with discrimination and dispassion, he should keep the disciple near him and slowly instruct him.

DEVOTEE: How can one make the mind one-pointed?

MAHARAJ: The practice of japam and meditation are the means of concentrating the mind. *Pranayama* [breath control] is also a means, but it is not safe for householders. Pranayama demands strict continence. Otherwise it may cause diseases. Those who practice pranayama should have nutritious food, pure air, and a suitable place. But meditation is not subject to any condition. Meditate in a solitary place. Practicing meditation for an hour or two a day is not enough. The longer you practice, the more your mind will become one-pointed toward God. Follow a routine with regularity. Whenever you find a quiet place or a place with scenic beauty, sit down for meditation. Seek God. Shun lust and gold and make him your mainstay. First renounce internally. If you withdraw your mind from the impermanent worldly objects, external renunciation will come automatically.

DEVOTEE: Maharaj, what is the meaning of the Vedantic saying, "Brahman alone is real and the world is unreal?"

MAHARAJ: It means that the world we see is apparent and not real. In samadhi the world disappears and one experiences uninterrupted bliss similar to the joy one gets after deep sleep. The sages expressed their experience of samadhi, saying, "Ananda, ananda, bliss, bliss." They could not say anything else. In that state there is no "I" or "you" but only Satchidananda—Existence-Knowledge-Bliss Absolute. He is with form and is also formless, and again he is beyond form and formlessness.

DEVOTEE: Maharaj, what is the proof of God's existence?

MAHARAJ: The seers have said, "We have seen God, and if you follow this way you will also see him." The Master used to say: "Merely by saying 'hemp, hemp' you will not be intoxicated. You must procure hemp, prepare it, take it, and then wait a little while. Gradually you will get intoxicated." Merely by saying "God, God" you will not realize him. Practice disciplines and then wait for his grace. You will see him in time.

DEVOTEE: Maharaj, sometimes while practicing japam the mind becomes blank. What causes that?

MAHARAJ: Patanjali [the author of the Yoga Sutras] mentioned this as an obstacle to yoga. Meditation is an uninterrupted flow of thought toward God. When meditation ripens, the vision of God comes, and then comes samadhi. The current of bliss continues for a long time after samadhi. Some say it continues throughout one's life.

Sri Chaitanya sent one of his disciples to Rai Ramananda. The disciple found him rolling in luxury. But as soon as Ramananda started talking about God, love overflowed from his heart.

14

JAPAM AND MEDITATION—THE GURU—HOLY COMPANY—ROUTINE—MORALITY

Place: Sri Ramakrishna Advaita Ashrama, Varanasi
Date: February 27, 1914

Swami Brahmananda asked a devotee: Do you pray or meditate?

DEVOTEE: No, Maharaj, I don't do either.

MAHARAJ: It is better to do a little every day. That will give you peace of mind and steadiness. Don't you have a family guru? Have you not yet received a mantram? It is good to be initiated. Practice japam and meditation regularly. Buy a rosary and repeat your mantram with it 108 to 1000 times. If you wish, repeat it more.

DEVOTEE: Maharaj, what shall I repeat?

MAHARAJ: Repeat the holy name of that form of God whom you love and respect most. You can meditate on his form as being either inside the heart or outside.

DEVOTEE: Meditation is not possible without a form. What form shall I choose?

MAHARAJ: A real guru, through meditation, can see the Chosen Deity of a disciple, and he instructs him accordingly. Then there is mental worship. As in external worship people offer flowers and sandal paste and perform arati [vespers], so in mental worship, while meditating on the form of God one mentally makes all those offerings.

Do not waste your time anymore! Start this very evening. You do not have to perform mental worship right now. Practice japam and meditation in the morning and evening. Follow what I say for two years. You will get bliss, ecstasy, and vision. In time I shall tell you what other practices you should take up.

Purchase an *asana* [meditation rug]. Use it only for worship and meditation. I think the garden adjacent to your house is quite solitary. If your house is noisy or if it is not convenient to practice there, then practice your disciplines in the garden. Moreover, a holy place like Varanasi is congenial for rapid spiritual progress. Practice my instructions for two years. Some get results quickly, and you may achieve your goal within a year. Start right now. After some days you will get so much bliss you won't want to leave your seat. A desire will come to meditate more. Sit erect and cross-legged, placing the hands either on the chest or in the lap.

Now and then have the company of the holy. Sometimes study the scriptures, and visit me when you can. Do not begin your meditation as soon as you sit on the asana. Sit silently for a couple of minutes or so and try to make the mind blank so that no distracting thought can arise. Then begin meditation. Rigidly follow this method for a couple of years. Thereafter meditation will become natural to you. If on any day you are hard-pressed with work, you should practice only once or try to finish your sadhana within ten or fifteen minutes. If even that is not possible, then think of the Lord once and bow down to him.

Get up early in the morning. Wash yourself, change your cloth, and sit down for meditation. Sprinkle a little Ganga water on your head. Follow the same routine in the evening. I assure you once more, if you follow what I have said, you will get peace of mind and live happily in this world.

Regarding moral conduct, please observe these two rules: First, always speak the truth; and second, look on every woman as your mother. These two moral virtues will take care of everything. Have sincere devotion for God. Never think that God does not exist. I tell you, God *is*. So start your spiritual journey today. Do not be wishy-washy anymore. I am still here. I shall tell you what to do next.

15

SELF-SURRENDER—BE SINCERE—FAITH IN THE GURU— GRACE—HOLD TO THE TRUTH—GOD IS INFINITE— KNOWLEDGE—KNOW GOD ALONE

Place: Belur Math
Year: 1914

MAHARAJ: Sri Ramakrishna used to say, "God reveals himself to a devotee who feels drawn to him by the combined force of these three attractions: the worldly man's attraction for possessions, the child's attraction for its mother, and the husband's attraction for his chaste wife." What does this mean? It means that when intense longing for God replaces all worldly desires of the mind, one realizes him, and gets his vision and divine touch. Sri Krishna said in the Gita, "Abandoning all duties, take refuge in me alone" [18.66].

Self-surrender, self-surrender, self-surrender—there is no other way. In this *kali yuga* [iron age] human beings are short-lived and depend on food. They have to do many things in this short span of life. People have very little energy, strength, renunciation, forbearance, or courage. Their minds are weak and they naturally run after enjoyments. In spite of all these handicaps, one will have to realize God. Otherwise this precious life will pass in vain without one's accomplishing anything. Surrender to God and wait for his grace—that is the easiest way in this age.

What do we understand by the word *self-surrender*? Does it mean that we do not have to do anything—that [we can attain God] without moving our hands or feet? No, it is not [so]. [We should] always sincerely pray: "O Lord, I do not know what is good and what is bad. I am solely dependent on you. [Give] me all that I need. Take me along the path that will bring me the greatest good. Grant me purity and strength so that I may have constant recollectedness of you."

Is it so easy to surrender oneself to God? Verbally many say: "We have surrendered ourselves to God. We are doing what he is making us do." But when we observe their lives, we see that their actions are quite contrary to what they say. If they do anything good, they take the credit for it themselves. They say with pride, "We did it, we did it." But if there is any mishap, they blame God and say, "He is giving us trouble and suffering." Most people behave this way.

We judge people by seeing their exteriors, but God is all-knowing and he looks into their minds. He rushes to that person who calls on him sincerely even once. Be simple. Unite your mind and speech. There is no partiality in his kingdom.

The Master used to say: "I have practiced all sixteen parts. Now you do only one-sixteenth." He has made spiritual life easy for us, but we are so lazy, hypocritical, and self-deceiving that we are incapable of doing anything. We cannot even put ready-made food into our mouths. When some people ask me for a blessing, I laugh to myself. They do not do as I say. The moment they leave my presence, they do whatever they like and think themselves clever or wise. If I ask them, "Did you follow what I told you to do?" some say, "We don't have time," and others say, "We are weak and sinners, so it is not possible to follow what you said." If you have no faith or desire to obey, then do whatever you want. These people want realization without doing anything.

When such people come to me, I pass the time telling jokes and silly stories. Why should I tire myself giving spiritual instructions to insincere people? Those I consider sincere and obedient, I instruct, and they try to practice accordingly. Deception becomes a habit when a person practices it from childhood. He wants to achieve everything without properly exerting himself.

There is no dearth of divine grace. People are not eager to receive God's grace, nor have they eyes to see his mercy. They only speak big words. Who wants God? Many people spend their lives talking high philosophy, but few practice religion. "Gurus are available by hundreds, but rare indeed is a true disciple." There are many people around to give advice, but who will follow it? Miseries and doubts cease for that person who follows the teachings of his guru with faith and love. He will not have to run here and there with a restless mind. God supplies all his needs and guides him in the right direction, holding his hand. There need be no anxiety for the one who has been blessed in this way.

One among millions of people is endowed with noble desires, sublime thoughts, and good qualities. And again among such great souls only a few can stick to their ideals to the last. Those persons in whose minds good thoughts have already sprung up should try their utmost to strengthen them and make them permanent. Pray unceasingly: "Lord, bestow your grace on me. Give me strength so that I can realize you."

Sri Ramakrishna used to say: "A maidservant in the house of a rich man always talks about the master's things as hers. But in her own mind she knows very well that they do not belong to her at all." Like that, as long as we are in this world we have to perform our duties, but we must know in our heart of hearts that this world is not our permanent home. It is only a temporary abode. Our real home is God, and we shall strive to return there at any cost.

Who wants to hold to the Truth or God? Everyone thinks that he is infallible and his way is the only way to salvation. Puffed up with pride, a person sometimes raises himself onto such a high pedestal that he even totally denies the existence of God. Do you know what he says? "I do not accept what I cannot understand." He has not the least inclination to understand how limited his power of comprehension is. What he thinks right one day he gives up as false the next. Thus he is continually changing his views. Intending to show the vastness of his knowledge, he really shows only that he does not care for anything or anybody. The Divine Mother alone knows in how many ways such a person is deluded.

We have realized that trying to limit the nature of God is foolishness. He is infinite and beyond the mind and intellect. That person alone to whom God is pleased to reveal his mysteries, can see, know, and understand. When one realizes God, the veils of ignorance disappear and the knots of one's heart become loosened. When a person reaches that state, he realizes, "I belong to God, and he is my own."

A person cannot attain any knowledge unless the Divine Mother supplies it. When she, out of mercy, removes the veil of maya, a person solves the mysteries of this world and the next. The intellect, as ordinarily understood, is not the real intellect. Its area or range is very limited. Those who want to attain true bliss in this life and solve its intricate problems such as "Who am I?" "Why am I here?" "What is the cause of my suffering?" "Why are some people like God and some like brutes?"—they must know God at any cost. Life's perplexing problems will be solved the moment he is realized.

Children love to hold onto a pole while twirling fast around it. Do you know where their attention is at that time? It is on the pole. They know very well that if they loosen their grip, they will fall and be injured. But there is no fear of falling as long as they hold tightly to the pole, and they may go on twirling around it as many times as they like. Similarly, you will have to know God first and hold to him firmly, as the children hold onto the pole. God is your pole. Holding him, whatever you do will be right, and there will be no fall or false step. Then it will not matter whether you follow the path of knowledge or devotion or action. Your life will do good to humanity. Blessed will be your life on earth.

16

CHARACTER-BUILDING—THE PARLOR OF GOD—
PURITY—BOOK LEARNING AND SPIRITUAL LIFE—
MONEY—RENUNCIATION—THREE RARE TREASURES—
FAITH—GRACE—PERSEVERANCE

Place: Shashi Niketan, Puri, Orissa
Year: 1915

MAHARAJ (*to a young man*): Some people have the desire to do philanthropic work. But I think one cannot do good to others unless one's own character is formed. Those who have taken refuge in God and have received his grace never make any mistake. Their actions, speech, behavior—all bring good to the world and to people. The Master used to say: "If you touch the 'granny' you are safe.[1] First hold the post—God." In the beginning try to know God and strengthen your faith and devotion and then do whatever you want to do. Knowing him, if you perform action, you will not only find peace in yourself but will be able to share it with others.

Sri Ramakrishna used to say, "The heart of a devotee is the

---

[1] An allusion to the Indian game of Hide and Seek. The leader is the "granny." She blindfolds the players and then hides. If any player can touch her, his blindfold is removed and he is released from the game.

parlor of God." If we want to introduce ourselves as Sri Ramakrishna's devotees or servants or children, we will have to be pure. God dwells in the pure heart. Our hearts will be his parlor when we have made them clean and pure.

God reflects on the pure mind. As a person's face is not reflected on a dirty mirror, so God is not reflected on an impure mind. You are still young and your mind is free from bad impressions. This is the time for you to make a seat for the Lord in your heart. Be pure and realize him in this life.

What will you achieve from book learning? It is not enough to have B.A. and M.A. degrees or to earn money as a lawyer. These accomplishments will give you momentary joy and nothing more. They will not help you achieve the goal [God-realization] of your life. That does not mean I want you to be illiterate. Religion is not for dull-witted people. They cannot grasp high ideals. Let those who want wordly enjoyments have degrees. Degrees will help them earn more money. Those who want the infinite bliss of God don't need many degrees. A person devotes a great deal of time in studying for a degree. If he would devote one-twelfth of that time in studying the scriptures, he would imbibe many lofty ideas. The Master used to say, "Books are like knots." Book learning inflates the ego and binds the soul. But this is not applicable to good books such as the Upanishads, the Gita, and Ramakrishna-Vivekananda literature. Read those books which enhance love and devotion for God. Reading only secular books increases conceit and takes people away from God. My boy, if you want your own welfare, be absorbed in the name of God. Do not be superficial. Dive deep. "Do or die"—let this be your motto!

Having too much money creates the same problem. It inflates the ego and takes a person away from God. Too much wealth breeds various kinds of evil in this world. Sri Ramakrishna could not touch money. He demonstrated in this present age true renunciation, which is the goal of human life. Ordinary people chase after worldly enjoyments like animals. If you want to be a real human being, take recourse to renunciation. Surrender yourself to God and realize him. Shun momentary pleasures for infinite bliss.

Don't you see in Sri Ramakrishna's blazing life what true renunciation is? O man, give up worldly desires and take refuge in God. Be aware of your real Self.

Renunciation alone can give a person peace. Give up everything for God. Make him your own. He is your father, mother, brother, friend, your all in all. When we have renounced mundane things and spent our time in recollectedness of him and meditation, then and then only shall we be real human beings and attain true bliss. This bliss cannot be expressed! Only that person knows who has tasted it.

Three things are necessary for God-realization: first, human birth; second, the desire for liberation; and third, association with a great soul. Now, by the grace of God you have all three. Build your life in such a way that it may not pass in vain. What will you gain by running after momentary enjoyments? Remember! You may be born again as a man, and you may have the desire for liberation, but you will not get the holy association of the disciples of Sri Ramakrishna. It is really rare to get the company of a great soul. This privilege comes to a person due to his good karma and austerity of his past life.

Faith, faith, faith! Have faith in the words of your guru and follow his instructions, and you will achieve everything. As a kitten surrenders to its mother, so surrender to your guru. He will make you do what is right for you. How much do you know about yourself? If you surrender to your guru, he will take responsibility for you. He will think of you and protect you from all trials and tribulations. As long as a person has not realized God, there is every possibility of his making mistakes. This does not happen, though, if one lives under the shelter of a guru. The Master used to say, "It is rather easy for a child to stumble if he holds his father's hand, but there can be no such fear if the father holds the child's hand."

Keep this in mind: As you have understood, by the grace of God, that your goal is God-realization, never deviate from this principle whether you are praised or blamed, whether your body survives or dies. For realizing the ideal, be ready to forbear all sufferings and afflictions. If you can form your character in this way, then only will you be a real person, a true follower of Sri Ramakrishna, and your association with the holy will have been effective.

Work hard. Give up all doubts and try to assimilate the teachings of your guru into your life. Do not publicize your spiritual life by beating drums. Practice your disciplines secretly so that people may not know about them. There are various types of people in this world. Some may destroy your spiritual mood through criticism, and some may inflate your ego by praising your efforts. Remember this saying of Sri Ramakrishna's: "To meditate, you should withdraw within yourself or retire to a secluded corner or to the forest." Devote yourself wholeheartedly to meditation for some days, and undoubtedly you will get bliss. You will be astonished, seeing your own transformation. Take a vow: "I must realize God in this life." You have come under the shelter of a real guru. Don't worry. You will succeed.

17

GOD IS THE WISH-FULFILLING TREE—DISCRIMINATION AND RENUNCIATION—PRAY TO GOD WITH HEART AND SOUL—SELF-EFFORT AND DIVINE GRACE

Place: Bhadrak, Orissa
Year: 1915

MAHARAJ: God is the kalpataru [the wish-fulfilling tree]. Whatever one asks from him, one gets. One gets what one desires. It is a tragedy that having obtained the rare privilege of a human birth, a person does not properly utilize it. Instead of fixing the mind on God, he is engrossed in worthless, mundane things, and yet he thinks, "I am happy." God also readily assents, "Be happy." Again, when that person suffers and laments, "Alas! What have I done in my life?" God immediately responds: "It is true. What have you done?" We are seated beneath the wish-fulfilling tree. What we want we will get—whether it is spirituality or sensuality.

God has given human beings two things—*vidya* [knowledge] and *avidya* [ignorance]. Vidya is of two kinds—discrimination and renunciation. The influence of these two leads a person toward God. Avidya is of six kinds—lust, anger, greed, infatuation, egoism, and jealousy. Their influence leads a person to the level of the brute. Cultivation of knowledge destroys ignorance, whereas cultivation of ignorance strengthens the idea of "I" and "mine" and binds a person to this world. Thus, ignorance takes human beings away from God and causes unending pain and suffering. Not only did God endow human beings with knowledge and ignorance, but he also gave them the power to discriminate between the two. Let a person select the good one and reap the result.

It is a great mistake for a person to blame God for his sufferings. You have selected your path according to your own liking, and you will now enjoy the consequences. You have no right to blame God. You are so much infatuated with momentary enjoyments that you forget everything, even how to discriminate between right and wrong. If you put your hand into the fire, it will be burned. Is it the fire's fault or yours? The Master used to say: "The nature of a lamp is to shed light. One man may read the Bhagavatam by the light of a lamp, and another may commit a forgery by the same light. Is the light responsible for that?" Likewise, God has placed before human beings two paths—good and bad. Choose as you please.

As is a person's meditation, so is his gain. If you take the course of discrimination and renunciation, you will realize God and inherit infinite bliss. On the other hand, if you follow the path of the world, you may enjoy momentary pleasures, but your future life will be steeped in darkness and you will have to pass through endless suffering. Where there is pleasure there is pain. Whether you like it or not, if you seek one you get the other along with it.

Sri Ramakrishna used to say: "The *malaya* breeze turns those trees which have some substance into sandalwood. But the unsubstantial trees, such as bamboo and banana, do not change." There are two classes of human beings in this world. Those in the first class imbibe the spirit of discrimination and renunciation as soon as they hear spiritual discourses. They regard worldly pleasures as trifling, and they long for the grace of God. They resolve to realize God and unveil the mystery of life and death. Forgetting the body idea, they begin sadhana with great zeal and in the end they succeed. The second class of people cannot be awakened in spite of being reminded of the highest ideal of life. Those in this class think that they will live forever and that without them the world cannot go on.

Moreover, they think it is foolish not to enjoy the available pleasurable objects. In this way they drag themselves down to the depths of ignorance and misery.

First try to understand which is better: the sweet fragrance of sandalwood or the foul odor of filth—peace or anxiety. Decide exactly what you want. Time is flowing away like a swift stream. It will be of no avail to cry over the past. Once time is gone it never returns. Therefore make the best use of the present without wasting a single moment. Train your mind in such a way that you constantly think of God and nothing else. Your days in this world are numbered and are running out fast. Do not spend your time in vain.

Pray to the Lord with heart and soul: "Lord, give me right understanding and make me your own. Remove the idea of 'I' and 'mine' from me. I have suffered terribly because of my ego. Lord, give me the knowledge that you are the doer and everything is yours." Is there anything you can call your own at the moment of death? Neither your possessions nor your relatives will go with you. Leaving everything behind, you will have to go to an unknown place. The more you say "I" and "mine," the more you chain yourself. What is there in this world for which people exert themselves their whole lives? When death approaches, can anybody protect a person?

A human birth is rare, and the goal of life is God-realization. What greater misfortune can befall you than to leave unfulfilled the purpose for which you have taken this birth? Make a tremendous effort and pray to God with earnest devotion that you may reach the goal.

Have you not heard how Sri Ramakrishna would cry at Dakshineswar? He used to say, "Mother, another day is gone in vain; still thou art not revealed unto me." Call on God with intense yearning. What is this world but an abode of misery? You have spent most of your days here in sorrow and trouble. Do you wish to do the same hereafter as well?

As you have come under the shelter of Sri Ramakrishna, then know for certain that you have received his grace. It will be really unfortunate if, having his grace, you cannot realize him or you fail to solve the riddle of life and death and obtain eternal bliss. You have been born in this age of Sri Ramakrishna. Now take advantage of his spirit. No one in any age has shown the path in such a simple and easy manner as Sri Ramakrishna has done. If you miss this opportunity, you will have to suffer a long time.

Unfurl the sail of your boat and move forward. Sri Ramakrishna is waiting. As soon as you unfurl the sail he will take your boat to the goal. Arise and awake! Infinite power is within you. Have faith in yourself and say: "I have heard his name and taken shelter in him. There cannot be any fear or weakness in me. By his grace I shall realize him in this very life." Do not look back. Go forward. Having his vision, achieve the purpose of your life and enjoy divine bliss.

18

RESTLESSNESS OF THE MIND—MEDITATION—DOES ṢRI RAMAKRISHNA EXIST?

Place: Belur Math
Date: December 1915

QUESTION: Sometimes when I sit for meditation the mind calms down easily. But at other times I fail to control it in spite of a thousand efforts. It flits about here and there all the time.

MAHARAJ: My boy, you are aware of the ebb tide and flood tide of the Ganga. Similarly, everything has its ebb and flow. The same law exists in spiritual practice, but you will notice it only in the initial stage. Don't worry about it. Be up and doing. If you continue your spiritual disciplines regularly for some time, there will no longer be an ebb or flow but rather an even tenor in your life.

You should not start japam and meditation as soon as you sit on the asana. At first you should withdraw your mind from external objects with the help of discrimination, and then begin japam and meditation. If you practice in this way for some days, the mind will gradually become concentrated.

Whenever you notice that the mind is becoming composed, leave all your work and meditate. And when you find that you have no taste for meditation or that the mind is not settling down, take your seat anyhow at the regular hour and try to concentrate your mind with the help of discrimination. Is it possible to calm the mind completely? Struggle, struggle, struggle! You will have to struggle every moment. If you continue your struggle, then the mind, the intellect, and the senses will come under your control.

QUESTION: Maharaj, does Sri Ramakrishna exist even now?

MAHARAJ: I see you have lost your mind. Having renounced hearth and home, why are we leading such a life? He exists always. Pray to him day and night for his vision. He will dispel all your doubts and will make you understand his true nature.

QUESTION: Do you see the Master nowadays?

MAHARAJ: Yes, I see him whenever he shows himself out of his mercy. Anybody who has his grace can see him. But how many people have that love and longing to see him?

19

SRI RAMAKRISHNA—REMEMBRANCE OF GOD

Place: Belur Math
Date: December 1915

MAHARAJ: Like the current of a river, the minds of ordinary people always flow toward lust and gold, name and fame. This ebb tide is to be diverted and the thought-current guided toward God. The natural abode of the Master's mind was the *turiya* plane [the transcendental realm]. He had to drag his mind forcibly toward the world. When he was practicing spiritual disciplines in the Panchavati, his mind always dwelt in that highest plane. Whenever his mind came down a little, somebody nearby would thrust a morsel of food into his mouth. Thus he was forcibly fed perhaps seven or eight mouthfuls of food in a day.

Unceasingly cultivate remembrance of God. If a person becomes adept in that, then when he sits for meditation he immediately becomes absorbed. The more meditation deepens, the more joy comes from within. Lust and gold then seem insipid. For that reason, one must uncompromisingly shun bad thoughts and vain talk. Bad thoughts dissipate energy. The Mundaka Upanishad says, "Give up all other [worldly] talk" [2.2.5]. Meditate on the Atman alone. That is the way to liberation. Ramprasad [a mystic] said: "When you lie down, think that you are prostrating before the Divine Mother; in sleep, imagine you are meditating on her; and when you go round the city, think that you are circumambulating Mother Shyama." The Bhagavad Gita also states: "Fix your mind on Me, be devoted to Me, sacrifice to Me, bow down to Me" [18.65]. This is the means of realizing God. The Master used to say, "One should not dissipate one's mental energy." That is, one must think of God and repeat his name. A worldly person takes so much care not to misuse a penny, but he is not aware of how much mental energy he misuses every day!

20

SELF-CONTROL—GOD IS—MEDITATION— EARNESTNESS—LONGING

Place: Belur Math
Date: December 1915

Swamis Brahmananda, Premananda, Shivananda, Subodhananda, and others were at that time staying at Belur Math. Some time earlier Swami Brahmananda had made a rule that all monks and brahmacharins (novitiates) were to rise at four in the morning and sit for meditation at half past four after finishing their bath. After a couple of hours' meditation, there would be singing of bhajans (devotional songs) for an hour in his room. In order to wake up the young monks punctually, the swami himself would get up before four o'clock and ask one of his attendants to ring the bell at ten minutes past four. On some days when the devotional singing was over, Swami Brahmananda would talk about spiritual life.

MAHARAJ: The mind, the ruler of the senses, has to be controlled. Again, both the mind and the intellect have to be merged in the Atman. Without cessation of the mind's thought-waves samadhi is not possible. It is the power of holy company that keeps the senses under control, but that does not mean the senses are dead. The cravings of the senses persist until samadhi is attained. If you loosen your hold on the senses a little, they will hiss at you with redoubled vigor. Therefore you have to be very careful until you go beyond the mind and the intellect.

God exists. *Dharma* [religion] exists—these are not mere words aimed at protecting the morality of the people. Truly God exists, and he can be directly experienced and realized. There is nothing truer than he. Fanaticism is horrible. Be calm, steady, and disciplined.

Practice meditation four times a day—in the early morning, after bathing, in the evening, and at midnight. Forsaking your hearth and home you have come here for God-realization. Now, with one-pointed devotion you must strive to achieve that. You will have to be restless for God like a mad dog. Your life will be miserable if you just live in this monastery content with bare necessities. You will neither gain anything in the world nor in spiritual life. There is a saying, "Catch at the shadow and lose the substance." Even if the mind refuses to dwell on God, you must keep up your practice. Read one chapter of the Bhagavad Gita every day. I have seen in my own life that when the mind goes down to the lower plane, the study of the Gita rouses the mind to the higher plane, immediately sweeping away all bad thoughts. An easygoing life is dangerous for seekers of God.

Poke your mind every day, asking: "Why have I come here? How have I spent the day? Do I really want God? And if I want him, then what am I doing to get him?" Place your hand on your heart and ask yourself whether or not you are sincerely working to realize God. The mind will try to play tricks. You will have to subdue it so that it does not deceive you. Hold onto the Truth and be pure. The purer you grow, the more you will acquire the power of concentration, and you will then be able to detect subtle tricks of the mind and annihilate them. "Who are your enemies? Your senses. But again they become your friends when they are conquered." Your undisciplined mind is your enemy and your disciplined mind is your friend. The more you can remove the impurities of the mind through self-examination, the more you will move forward in the spiritual realm.

Practice japam and meditation intensely. At first the mind dwells on gross objects, but when the mind becomes disciplined through meditation, it learns to grasp finer things. Winter is the best season for japam and meditation, and youth is the best time. Go and sit for meditation taking a vow like Buddha: "Let my body be dried up on this seat. Without attaining illumination I shall not move from this place." Why don't you find out for yourself whether God truly exists or not?

It is good to practice a little forbearance, such as taking one meal on the day of the new moon and on the eleventh day of the fortnight. Instead of spending time in idle talk and gossip, remember God all during the day. Practice feeling the presence of God in every action and in every moment of your life. This will gradually awaken the kundalini power. Is there any discipline higher than remembrance of God? The veils of maya will be lifted one after another, and you will see what a glorious thing abides within you. Your Self will shine forth and you will be Self-revealed.

The days are passing one after another, and what are you doing? These days will never return. Pray to Sri Ramakrishna. He is present still. If you call on him sincerely, he will show you the way and lead you to the goal. Don't forsake him or you will be ruined. Cultivate this mood: "Master, you are mine and I am yours." After embracing this spiritual life, if you do not practice japam and meditation, or if you do not try to become absorbed in God, you will face endless suffering. The mind will always dwell on lust and gold. It is good to have a feeling of *tamas* [obstinacy] springing from *sattva* [calmness]: "Alas! I have not yet found God. What is the use of this wretched life? I shall end it now."

The bearing of the monks at Rishikesh is like that of free souls, but in reality they have not reached that stage. They only delight in debating about God and the scriptures.

21

FREE WILL—WILLPOWER—COMPREHENDING THE INFINITE

Place: Belur Math
Date: January 7, 1916

A DOCTOR: Maharaj, is it not due to samskaras [impressions] that of two persons born and brought up in the same family, one becomes a monk and the other an immoral person?

MAHARAJ: Everything is free will. The first person willed to be a monk, so gradually his will became stronger and he became a monk. The second one developed his will differently, so he became different.

DOCTOR: A young chicken does not jump into the water but it is afraid of the eagle, whereas a young duck jumps into the water. Is this not due to the samskaras of their past lives?

MAHARAJ: It is hard to explain. When the young duck is in the egg, it does not rush to the water, and again in the beginning the young chickens are not afraid of the eagle. When their free will grows, fear comes. Young children try to grab hold of fire. Later, when their free will develops and they learn to discriminate between what is harmful and what is harmless, they desist from that action. Look at your daily life. You are sick and your body is moving toward destruction. Your free will resolves to protect it through medicine. As a result your body lasts for some more years. Thus creation, preservation, and destruction are going on through free will.

What is the purpose of spiritual disciplines? To develop free will. The more one strengthens one's willpower, the more one moves toward God. The Master used to say, "Awaken your inner power." Success does not come to souls who are weak-minded.

The more one's mind becomes pure, the more one's willpower increases. Look at Buddha. Sitting under the Bo-tree he resolved, "Either my body will be dried up on this seat or I shall attain nirvana [liberation]." And he attained it because he had tremendous willpower. This law is applicable everywhere. Monks and devotees should always try to increase their willpower. One should resolve to realize God in this very life. Don't procrastinate or be wishy-washy. Your willpower is guiding you. You wished that your body would move from one place to another, so your body moved. First your will dictated, then your action followed. . . .

DOCTOR: From where does willpower come?

MAHARAJ: It is a difficult question, and there are many things to say about it. There is no free will in a dead body. A dead body cannot wish or move. Let us stop here for today. Tomorrow I shall take your side and prove there is no such thing as samskaras or willpower.

Let me tell you something important. You may not understand now but you will in the future. Please remember this: The mind and the intellect of each person are pushing him toward the path of good and not toward evil. God is guiding some through thorns, some directly, and some through other ways. There is a kind of discipline: Turn the mind free and let it go wherever it wants to go and do whatever it wants to do. You will notice that in the beginning the mind may move to the wrong path, but eventually it will move back to the right path. Don't forget this. Keep it in mind.

It is impertinence for us to talk about God. We limit him when we try to express him through the mind and speech.

There is a beautiful verse in the *Shiva Mahimnah Stotram*: "If the goddess of learning were to write eternally, having the biggest branch of the celestial tree for her pen, the whole earth for paper, the blue mountain for ink, and the ocean for an inkpot, even then, O Lord, thy attributes could not be fully described."

Before the Master passed away in the Cossipore garden, he would tell us about his visions of the Infinite. One day Girish and Swamis Vivekananda, Ramakrishnananda, Niranjanananda, and I were present in his room. We were then young boys, but Girish was elderly and extremely intelligent. Hearing a few words about the Infinite from the Master, Girish exclaimed: "Sir, don't talk anymore. I get dizzy." Oh, what a conversation! The Master used to say: "Shukadeva is like an ant which is satisfied with a small particle of sugar. Rama, Krishna, and other Incarnations are like bunches of grapes hanging on the tree of Satchidananda." These are mere thoughts about the Infinite. It is hard to comprehend.

22

RELIEF WORK—BRAHMACHARYA—STUDY—WORK AND WORSHIP—SELFLESS ACTION

Place: Belur Math
Date: February 2, 1916

Swamis Brahmananda, Premananda, and Saradananda were present in the Belur monastery. A monk announced in the dining hall that there would be a meeting at four o'clock that afternoon in Swami Brahmananda's quarters, and he asked that all monastics be present. The meeting began on time.

A monk asked Swami Brahmananda: Maharaj, the young monks do not like to get involved in relief work. How can we continue our mission program?

MAHARAJ: Who does not want to work?

When the name of a particular monk was mentioned, the swami addressed him directly, saying: Why don't you take part in relief work?

MONK: There is no opportunity and time left for spiritual practices if one is busy most of the day with relief operations.

MAHARAJ: Does relief work continually demand long hours?

MONK: No, Maharaj. In the beginning, though, it is a very laborious job.

MAHARAJ: Then why do you say that you don't get the time for meditation? Look, my boy, that type of excuse does not befit you. You are all monks and brahmacharins, and there is a power of brahmacharya within you. You will have to combine in your life both contemplation and action. Only a householder speaks this way, saying, "If I do this, I can't do that." I think you have no inclination for meditation. You spend your time working, chatting, and gossiping, and then give the excuse that you have no time left for meditation. I agree that in the beginning relief work is hard labor, but it does not continue for very long. So why don't you practice your spiritual disciplines? Don't you feel ashamed to talk that way?

At first we also worked hard for Sri Ramakrishna's Order. Though I was a monk I had to run to the offices of lawyers and legal advisors. [A monk is not supposed to be involved in worldly activities.] I don't feel that it did us any harm. We know that all duties are for the Master.

Hearing Swami Brahmananda's words, all kept quiet. Swami Saradananda then asked the monks to express their difficulties and problems. Nobody dared say anything, and finally Maharaj asked one monk: Do you have any complaint?

THE MONK: Previously I was not getting any chance to study the scriptures in the monastery, but now that I have put my mind in meditation, I don't have any difficulty.

ANOTHER MONK: There is no good arrangement for scriptural classes in the monastery. It would be nice if we could have a Sanskrit scholar.

MAHARAJ: Why? You are studying under Swami Atmananda. He is a Sanskrit scholar and a good monk.

* * *

Maharaj got up from his chair and continued: I vividly remember what Swamiji said to Turiyananda and me at Mount Abu before he left for America. He said, "Whatever you do for the good of the world and for the welfare of all—that is *dharma* [religion], and whatever you do for yourself—that is *adharma* [irreligion]." Oh! What a great message! These are all priceless words. Can anybody appreciate such words?

I hear that some of you are saying the activities of the Mission are obstacles to meditation, that relief work does not help spiritual progress, and moreover that Swami Premananda and I do not care for those activities. These notions of yours are completely wrong. You do not understand us. You must follow the ideal. I say again and again most emphatically that whatever relief work you do, you must also continue your japam and meditation in the morning and evening and after work. Often we used to hear from Swamiji, "Work and worship," which means, do your work and practice your meditation. Of course, if it happens that due to the pressure of work you cannot practice your disciplines for a day or two, that is a different matter. Can anybody practice japam and meditation twenty-four hours a day? Therefore you will have to perform unselfish action [*nishkama karma*]. If you do not do that, various bad thoughts and frivolous ideas will hover in your mind. So selfless action is better than inaction. The Bhagavad Gita and other scriptures stress this point, and I also speak from my own experience.

*   *   *

Don't you see what a great war is going on in Europe? Giving up their wives, children, and enjoyments, men are sacrificing their lives for their country. And you have also renounced your hearth and home for a greater ideal—God-realization and doing good to humanity. You have dedicated yourselves to the Master and still you abhor *karma yoga* [the path of selfless work]! Swamiji used to say: "If you think one life has gone in vain for doing good to others, let it go. How many lives you have spent idly! Why are you afraid of losing one life for doing good to humanity?" There is no need to be afraid. The scriptures say that selfless action leads to God-realization. The Gita says: "Verily, by action alone men like Janaka [a king and knower of Brahman] attained perfection" [3.20]. "A man who does his work without attachment attains the Highest" [3.19].

Swamiji once said: "Look. The boys who are coming now will not be able to practice japam and meditation day and night, so I have started these philanthropic activities." It really would be wonderful if somebody could pass the day and night in meditation, prayer, and study. But in fact they can't do it, so they resort to idleness. Good work cannot go in vain without bearing a result, and that result will clear the path for your liberation. I have observed that those monks who have returned from Rishikesh [a place for ascetics] after practicing austerities exclusively for three or four years are less advanced than those monks who are living in one particular place and doing both meditation and karma yoga. Know for certain, those who neglect their work are deceiving themselves.

23

REGULARITY IN SPIRITUAL LIFE—THE PLAY OF MAYA—CONTROL OF THE MIND—DO OR DIE

Place: Belur Math
Year: 1916

MAHARAJ: One should follow a routine in one's spiritual practices. Steadfast devotion is extremely important. Without it, no one can be successful in any work. You must have such steadfastness that wherever you are placed you feel compelled to observe your routine. Make a routine of everything. "I shall meditate so long, repeat my mantram so many times, study for so much time, and sleep so many hours." With an irregular life you cannot be successful in any work. A regulated life is the only means of physical and mental development. When a watch starts losing time, one regulates it. Then it gives the correct time. Similarly with the mind. For various reasons the mind becomes unsettled, but one can regulate it in holy company and give it a fresh start. One can avoid many troubles and obstacles if one tries to follow implicitly the instructions of holy people. By assimilating their teachings into one's life, one inherits the spiritual treasure they possess, and thus one becomes blessed.

Unless one can fix one's mind on God it is difficult to protect oneself from the whirlpool of the world. Nobody knows in how many ways Mahamaya [the Great Enchantress] plays her tricks! Trying to bear the brunt of it all wears out one's life. Is it an insignificant thing or a joke to save oneself from the constant struggle against such indomitable enemies as lust, anger, delusion, and so on? Unless one receives strength from God, one cannot escape the meshes of maya and thus move in safety. Therefore I tell you, boys, first get strength from him.

Rules are necessary as long as the mind is not under control. Unless you have a regular routine the mind will not allow you to do anything. It will always prompt you to loaf. If you follow a routine, you can command your mind: "Listen, mind. You are subject to this routine. Whether you like it or not, you will have to follow it." You have to bring the mind under control forcibly. And when the mind comes under your control, all routine will fall away by itself.

Life is flowing away like the water of a river. The past day will never return. Make good use of your time, my boys. It will be of no use to lament at the end. Be up and doing! Do or die! Death is inevitable sooner or later. If one's life ends for the sake of God, there is only gain and no loss. Say to your mind resolutely, "I *must* realize God." Attach no importance to this world. Is there any happiness here? There is only sorrow and suffering. You have to go beyond grief and affliction. When one gets a glimpse of God, pleasures of the flesh become mere trash. That bliss is infinite. What is there to fear when you have taken shelter in the Master's place? Shun all ephemeral things and make the Master the pivot of your life.

24

PRIVATE INSTRUCTIONS—FAITH—BRAHMACHARYA—CONTROL OF THE TONGUE—KEEPING SPIRITUAL PRACTICES A SECRET—SLEEP

Place: Belur Math
Year: 1916

MAHARAJ: Regarding spiritual practices, the same rules cannot be applied to all. The guru must observe the tendencies of the disciple. If a person is instructed against his nature, that instruction injures him rather than benefits him. Therefore it is extremely important that the guru closely study the individual tendencies and peculiarities of his disciple and give instructions according to that person's nature and understanding.

A few things about spiritual life can be said openly, but personal instruction cannot be given in the presence of others. The Master used to call aside each disciple separately and instruct him according to his nature and competency. If you have any questions regarding spiritual practices, please ask your guru privately. Nevertheless, it is good for everyone to know a few basic things.

First, you must have firm faith in God. You must have conviction that if you realize God and receive his grace, all the problems of your life will be solved, the purpose of your coming to the world will be accomplished, and that by tasting the bliss of the eternal Brahman, you will be immortal.

Second, brahmacharya, or continence. Without brahmacharya, it is not possible for anyone to hold fast to a great ideal. If anyone wants to nourish the body, mind, and brain and develop them fully, that person must practice brahmacharya. Why did our teachers place so much stress on brahmacharya? Because they knew that if this vital point is weak, spiritual life falls apart. A brahmacharin does not waste his energy. He may not look like a wrestler, but day by day the power of his brain increases so much that he can easily grasp the transcendental truths.

Third, control of the tongue. The tongue can cause a lot of trouble. The Master used to say, "Keep your stomach and brain cool." If they are quiet one can accomplish a lot of work. Your brain gets heated when you talk for a long time and unnecessarily. As a result your mind becomes restless and you cannot practice meditation. You also don't get any sleep, and other complications arise.

Likewise, the glutton who has no restraint over his tongue injures his body and mind. Whenever he gets some choice food, he overeats and then suffers from breathing difficulty. His whole energy is spent in digesting that food, and if he cannot digest it he falls ill. Foods like onion, garlic, and chili excite the body and mind so much that later one finds it extremely difficult to bring the system under control. I think that those who want to lead a spiritual life should pay special attention to what they eat and drink. Don't overeat. Eat that food which is nutritious, easily digestible, and not exciting. Avoid stimulating food because it is injurious, and also avoid that food which increases tamas. What is the purpose of food? To maintain good health. And one needs good health for God-realization. The scriptures say, "Health, indeed, is the primary factor in spiritual practice." Maintain the good health of your body. That does not mean, however, that you must think of the body day and night.

Sri Ramakrishna used to say, "Eat as much as you like

during the day but eat sparingly at night." The idea is that the full meal taken at noon will be easily digested, and if you eat lightly at night, your body will remain light and you can easily concentrate the mind. A heavy meal at night produces laziness and sleep. How do you want to spend the night—in sleep or in meditation? People are generally busy during the day, so it is difficult to still the restless mind at that time. But at night nature becomes calm and all creatures go to sleep. This, therefore, is the best time for meditation. Concentration becomes quickly intensified in the quiet hours of the night.

Spiritual life is not a matter for public display. Such a thing harms an aspirant. People will ridicule and criticize him. They will give him free advice and confuse him, saying, "This one is not right, and that one is not right either," and create obstacles to his spiritual practices. Do you know the sign of a real aspirant? Everybody thinks he is sleeping under the mosquito curtain, but actually he is spending the whole night in meditation.

While young, one must try hard to get a taste of divine bliss. Once one tastes it, one gets intoxicated. Then one cannot give up God in spite of being threatened by others. It seems to me that those who have a problem with excessive sleep should sleep during the day and stay awake at night. The best times for meditation are the junctions between day and night, night and day, and at midnight. People usually misuse these precious hours.

The Master could seldom sleep at night. He did not allow the boys who lived with him to sleep either. When others had gone to bed he would wake up his disciples, saying: "What is this? Have you come here to sleep?" Then he would instruct each disciple and send him for meditation to the Panchavati, Kali temple, or Shiva temple, according to his inclination. After practicing japam and meditation as directed, each would return to the room and sleep. Thus the Master made his disciples work hard. Often he would say: "Three classes of people stay awake at night: the yogi, the enjoyer, and the sick person. You are all yogis, so sleeping at night is not meant for you."

25

KEEP YOUR EXPERIENCES PRIVATE—THE SPIRITUAL GUIDE—HOW TO CONQUER FEAR OF DEATH—HAVE FAITH IN YOURSELF—SIN

Place: Belur Math
Year: 1916

MAHARAJ: When the mind gets absorbed in spiritual disciplines, one experiences immense bliss within. As a result, days and nights pass unnoticed.

It is not good to speak to others about one's spiritual experiences, especially to those who are incompatible by nature. It ruins the spiritual mood. Of course it benefits an aspirant if he talks about spiritual life with a person of a similar nature. Fellow pilgrims can help each other. A person can escape danger on his journey if he gets acquainted with a traveler who already has followed that path and knows its problems. If you have a good guide, he will show you important things on the way and you will not have to face any troubles. Moreover, you will be able to accomplish your objective in a short time and reach your destination quickly. Man's intellect has its limitations, so one should live with a good teacher. Life is short but there are many things to do. One should strive hard to reach the goal within this short span of life.

Human life is unpredictable. It may end after twenty years or today. Nobody knows when it will end, so it is better to acquire something soon for the journey. Who knows when the call will come? If you go to an unknown land empty-handed you will suffer. Because you were born, you must die. It is true, after death you will have to go to a different place. At any cost, collect all provisions for that journey and keep yourself ready. When the call comes, start your journey with a smiling face. There will be no fear or anxiety if you know definitely that you have what you need for the way.

When you have the noble desire to realize God and an opportunity to lead a good life, please use it wholeheartedly and attain the Truth. Hold the pole [God] firmly. Let the body go, but don't give up the pole. Have faith in yourself. "I am a human being, and I can do everything"—have this kind of faith and move forward. You will reach the goal. Your life will be meaningful. Coming and going are painful. Stop this dreadful cycle of reincarnation. Be the Lord's eternal companion.

Remove all fear and weakness from your mind. Never debase yourself by thinking about sin. Sin, however great it may seem in the eyes of man, is nothing in the eyes of God. One glance of his can uproot sins of millions of births in a moment. In order to divert human beings from the path of sin, the scriptures mention heavy punishments for the sinner. Of course every action bears a result, and evil actions disturb one's peace of mind.

26

TIME FOR MEDITATION—THE NERVE-CURRENT—HOW TO CONTROL THE MIND—NONATTACHMENT—STRUGGLE—RECOLLECTEDNESS—THE MYSTERY OF GOD

Place: Balaram Mandir, Calcutta
Date:　January 30, 1918

It was seven o'clock on Sunday morning. Swami Brahmananda was sitting quietly in his small room. The monks, brahmacharins, and devotees came and took their seats after bowing down to him. Addressing them all, Maharaj said: It is good to rise very early. The best times for practicing self-control are when night passes into day and day passes into night. Nature is then very peaceful—a favorable condition for practicing japam and meditation. At these times the nerve-current flows through the *sushumna* [the hollow canal in the spinal column], and there is rhythmic respiration through both the nostrils. At other times the nerve-current flows through the *ida* [the left side of the spine] and the *pingala* [the right side of the spine], that is, respiration is through only one nostril at a time. The mind gets restless then. The yogis are alert to when the nerve-current is flowing through the sushumna. Noticing it they set aside all work and sit for meditation.

The mind can be controlled in two ways: First, one should go to a solitary place and concentrate the mind on a particular object by making it free from all other thoughts. Second, one should develop the mind by thinking good thoughts. As the cow must be given high-quality fodder to yield high-quality milk, so the mind has to be given the right kind of food in order to make it calm. The best food for the mind is meditation, japam, and noble thoughts.

There are some spiritual aspirants who allow the mind to wander at random and just watch what it does. When the mind in its restless movements cannot find peace anywhere, it at last turns to God of its own accord and takes shelter in him. If you watch your mind, the mind must inevitably watch you. It is therefore necessary to always watch the mind. A solitary place is very favorable for spiritual practice. For this reason the sages and seers loved the Himalayas and the banks of the Ganga.

True renunciation is the renunciation of desires. A person might have a thousand possessions, but as long as he is not attached to them he will be free. And again, a person might possess very little, but if he's attached to it he will be bound. God is reflected on the mind which has been purified by spiritual practices.

Struggle, struggle, struggle! That person is lifeless who does not struggle. The next stage after a joyous acceptance of this struggle is peace.

The easiest of all spiritual practices is the constant remembrance of God. One must know him to be one's very own. Just as one entertains and talks with one's relatives and friends, so one should act toward God within. This is how one attains peace.

Can anybody understand the Lord's work? He is infinite and again he is finite. He even appears as man. The legendary crow Bhushandi at first took Ramachandra to be a mere man, and consequently it found no place in the three worlds where it could take shelter. Later, through Rama's grace, it realized him to be God, and it pleased him by singing his praises.

The ways in which God guides people are incomprehensible. Sometimes he takes them along an easy path, sometimes through thorns, and sometimes across difficult hills and mountains. There is no other way than to resign oneself completely unto him.

27

HOW TO CONTROL THE MIND—MEDITATION—THE CHOSEN DEITY AND THE MANTRAM—JAPAM

Place: Balaram Mandir, Calcutta
Date: February 4, 1918

QUESTION: Maharaj, the other day you told me that the mind can be made steady in two ways. Could you tell me which one I should follow?

MAHARAJ: Hold the mind forcibly to the blessed feet of your Chosen Deity.

QUESTION: Where shall I concentrate on my Chosen Deity?

MAHARAJ: In the heart. Think that he is facing you while you are in meditation.[1]

QUESTION: The heart is covered with flesh, blood, and bone. How can I think of the Lord there?

MAHARAJ: Don't think about flesh, blood, and bone at all. Think that he is seated in the heart chakra [*anahata chakra*—the fourth center of consciousness]. In the beginning the thought of flesh, blood, and bone may come to your mind, but later the thought of the Chosen Deity will replace it.

QUESTION: Shall I meditate on the Chosen Deity exactly as I see him in his picture or image?

---

[1] Maharaj then gave the disciple detailed instructions which can only be learned personally from a guru. A monastic disciple of Swami Brahmananda once wrote to a brother disciple how Maharaj instructed him during initiation: "While doing japam, meditate on the illumined form of the Chosen Deity in the heart. Then practice meditation on the Chosen Deity without japam. Place the form of the Chosen Deity in the heart in such a way that his face will be toward your back, and his back will be toward your front. In this way, place the illumined form of the Chosen Deity in the heart and meditate. In deep meditation the form will disappear and only a light will remain, and then your mind will merge into that."

MAHARAJ: Yes. Meditate on the same form. But think of him as living, luminous, and blissful.

QUESTION: I have heard that one should, while repeating the mantram, think of its meaning. Would you tell me how? Should I think of the mantram letter by letter or as a whole?

MAHARAJ: Do you know what the meaning of the mantram is? It is like calling a person by his name. You have a name. As I call you, your form also comes to my mind. In the same way, while repeating the mantram, meditate on the Chosen Deity also.

QUESTION: How should one repeat the mantram—mentally or audibly?

MAHARAJ: When you practice your japam alone in solitude, repeat the mantram in such a way that only you can hear. And if anyone is nearby, repeat it mentally.

28

JAPAM—MEDITATION—THE POWER OF THE
MANTRAM—HOW TO CONTROL THE MIND

Place: Balaram Mandir, Calcutta
Date: February 6, 1918

QUESTION: When I sit for practicing japam I perceive the mantram in shining letters before my eyes. As soon as this happens, the Chosen Deity disappears and I see only the mantram in a luminous form. Please tell me what I should do.

MAHARAJ: It is a very good and auspicious sign. You are supposed to see both the mantram and the Chosen Deity. The mantram is the Sound-Brahman. Watch the mantram and at the same time try to visualize the Chosen Deity. [Sri Ramakrishna used to say, "The name and the person named are identical."]

QUESTION: How should I start to meditate on the Chosen Deity? Shall I begin with the face?

MAHARAJ: First make your salutations at his feet and after visualizing the feet, see other parts of his body.

QUESTION: Is there any special significance of a long mantram?

MAHARAJ: Yes, some mantras are long. The mantram is charged with spiritual power. Repeat it as many times as you can.

QUESTION: How can I control the mind?

MAHARAJ: Practice meditation every day. The best time for meditation is early in the morning. The mind gets concentrated quickly if one reads a little from the scriptures before meditating. After meditation one should sit at least half an hour, because at the time of meditation one may not immediately derive its desired effect. It may come a little later. For this reason an aspirant should not occupy himself with worldly thoughts or engage in secular affairs immediately after meditation. It may injure his spiritual growth.

It is absolutely necessary to practice japam and meditation regularly, even though you may not like it. Even mechanical practice is a great help. Repeat the mantram at least two hours a day. Sometimes it is beneficial just to sit quietly in a solitary garden, or on the bank of a river, or near a vast meadow, or alone in one's room. In the beginning one should establish a routine for spiritual practices, and one should not take on responsibilities which might jeopardize this routine.

29

MEDITATION—AUSPICIOUS DAYS FOR JAPAM—MORAL TEACHINGS—MEDITATION ON THE GURU

Place: Balaram Mandir, Calcutta
Date: February 9, 1918

QUESTION: What shall I do if while meditating on my Chosen Deity other forms of gods and goddesses appear before me?

MAHARAJ: Know it to be a very auspicious sign. At that time think that your Chosen Deity is appearing through those forms. He is one, and again he is many. Visualize your Chosen Deity, but if he appears before you in another form, enjoy that divine vision. After some days you will see that those forms will merge into your Chosen Deity.

Practice more japam on auspicious days, such as the day of the new moon and the full moon, the eighth day after the full or new moon, and days on which special celebrations are held.

You must look upon all women as your mother. [This instruction was given to a monastic disciple.] If you give your word to someone, keep it by all means. If you have any doubt about being able to keep a promise, then say, "I shall try."

QUESTION: I have heard that one should meditate on the guru before one meditates on God. I don't know how to do that. Could you tell me?

MAHARAJ: As you meditate on your Chosen Deity in the heart, similarly, before you begin your spiritual practices, meditate on your guru in the heart.[1] Think that the guru and the Chosen Deity are one. Then merge the form of the guru

---

[1] According to the Tantric tradition, a person is supposed to meditate on the guru in the head and then on the Chosen Deity in the heart. In some places Maharaj said to meditate on the guru in the head.

into the form of the Chosen Deity. After that repeat your mantram and meditate on the Chosen Deity.

30

THE PLAY OF MAYA—MEDITATION ON THE FORMLESS GOD

Place: Balaram Mandir, Calcutta
Date: June 21, 1918

It was nine o'clock on Wednesday morning. Swami Brahmananda was strolling in the big hall of Balaram Bose's house in Calcutta. A devotee from Dacca arrived and bowed down to the swami. Maharaj greeted the devotee and inquired about the monks and activities of the Ramakrishna center in Dacca. After a short while, Chunilal Basu, an old devotee of Sri Ramakrishna, also arrived.

MAHARAJ: Maya forces the mind to think lower thoughts. The Master used to say, "Even Brahman weeps, entrapped in the snare of the five elements." First practice spiritual disciplines vigorously and touch God. After that thousands of worldly affairs will not be able to overwhelm you.

A man entrapped by maya does not understand how painful it is to have a body in this world. This human body is not real. It is decaying day by day. Still he is not aware of it. Due to the influence of maya he forgets the goal of his life and suffers from birth and death again and again. It is really painful to have a body, but then God-realization is possible in this human life. So one should work in such a way that one will not have to be born again. Realize God by all means, and then only will you be able to transcend this cycle of birth and death.

QUESTION: Maharaj, how does one meditate on the formless God?

MAHARAJ: Only an advanced soul can meditate on the formless God. First concentrate on the gross form, then the subtle, then the causal, and at last concentrate on the Final Cause, which is the formless Brahman.

31

THE NATURE OF A HOLY PERSON

Place: Ramakrishnapur, Howrah, West Bengal
Date: August 1918

Swami Brahmananda was seated in the parlor. A young disciple arrived from Calcutta and bowed down to the swami. Maharaj asked him how the activities of the Students' Home were going.

THE YOUNG DISCIPLE: They are not going on well at all. There are various problems in the Students' Home.

MAHARAJ: Why did you not inform me before now?

The disciple could not give any suitable reply to the swami and sat there sadly.

MAHARAJ: Sometimes a person whom you help will harm you. Ishwar Chandra Vidyasagar, a great philanthropist, helped many people in his life, but later those people criticized and harmed him. At last he became disgusted. When he would hear from any of his friends that a certain person had criticized him, he would reply: "What? I did not give him any help!" That is the nature of a worldly person. But the nature of a holy person is different: He will continue to do good to people in spite of everything. The nature of an evil person is to do harm to others.

There was a holy man who used to practice meditation sitting on the bank of a river. One day he saw a scorpion being carried away by the current of the river. Out of compassion he grabbed hold of it and released it on the ground. As soon as he touched the scorpion it stung his hand, causing him terrible pain. After a while the scorpion fell back into the water and was again about to be carried away by the current. Again the monk rescued it and was stung by the ungrateful creature. A third time the scorpion fell into the river, and seeing its pitiable condition the compassionate monk started to rescue it. At that moment a bystander said to the monk: "Sir, I have been watching you. I saw how that scorpion stung you several times. Still you are trying to save its life?" The monk replied: "The nature of a scorpion is to sting, and the nature of a holy person is to do good to others, so I am following my nature. It is true the scorpion stung me, but that does not mean I must be cruel." Saying so, the monk picked up the scorpion once more and carried it to a distant place so that it could not again fall into the water. The nature of a holy man is to do good to the world, and he never gives up his divine nature.

32

REPEAT THE NAME OF THE LORD—PRAYER—GRACE—YEARNING—THE WORLDLY WAY—SURRENDER

Place: Belur Math
Year: 1918

MAHARAJ: God's name purifies the body and the mind. "I have taken the name of the Lord, so what have I to fear? What is there in the world to bind me? Repeating his name I have become immortal."—One should practice spiritual disciplines with this kind of faith.

What is the goal of spiritual practices? It is to realize God and attain his grace. Lust and gold pollute the mind. First remove all impurities which have accumulated in the mind through birth after birth; otherwise there will be no possibility of spiritual progress. One cannot attain God's grace without purifying the mind. Sri Ramakrishna used to cite a beautiful illustration: "If the needle is covered with mud, the magnet cannot attract it. But when the mud is washed off, the needle is naturally drawn to the magnet." Similarly, impurities of the mind are washed away if one thinks of and meditates on God and prays to him with tears and repentance: "Lord, forgive me. I will not do anything wrong anymore." Then God, who is like the magnet, draws to himself the mind, which is like the needle. The moment the mind becomes pure, divine grace flows and one obtains the vision of God.

The Master illustrated how the vision of God depends on his grace through this analogy: "The police sergeant goes on his rounds in the dark of night with a lantern[1] in his hand. No one sees his face. But with the help of that light the sergeant sees everyone else's face, and they too can see one another. If one wants to see the sergeant, however, one must say to him: 'Sir, please turn the light on your own face. Let me see you.' In the same way, one must pray to God, 'O Lord, be gracious and turn the light of knowledge on thyself, that I may see thy face.' He is the Sun of Knowledge. One can see God only if he turns his light toward his own face."

As long as a person has any craving for enjoyment he cannot

---

[1] A reference to the lantern carried by the nightwatch, which has dark glass on three sides.

have sincere yearning for realization or the vision of God. Children forget themselves while engrossed in their toys and sweets, but after awhile, when they tire of those things, they become restless and cry for their mother. Similarly, when a person is rid of desires for enjoyment, his mind longs for God and he thinks only about how to find him.

Is it an easy matter to raise noble desires in the mind? Know for certain that it is by a special grace of God that one has the desire to know him. In this realm of Mahamaya people receive innumerable blows and suffer untold miseries, but still they do not want to change their lives. If somebody offers good advice, they become angry. What a delusion! People know very well that if they put their hands into fire they will be burned. Still they do it again and again. Not only that, they invite others to do it also. If someone differs with their ideas, they call him crazy and even go to the length of persecuting him.

Have you not seen how elders put restrictions on a boy who wants to be a monk and lead a religious life? But they will not make sufficient efforts to rectify the boy if he goes astray and becomes a menace to himself and to society. All troubles begin when one treads the path of a virtuous life! Worldly people try their utmost to drag down a virtuous person to their own level.

Once the father of one of our monks came to the monastery and said: "I would have been happier if my son had died instead of becoming a monk. There is no control over death. One has to resign oneself and accept it. I had such great expectations of my son! As he has broken my trust, he will never prosper in spiritual life. If I had known that he would grow up to become a monk, I would have arranged for his death when he was born. Then I would have avoided all this pain." How terrible is this world! This man did not understand that if his son became a genuine monk, he would not only do good to himself but to his family also.

People lose their tempers over trifling causes. They don't have the patience to think deeply before they act. They object to whatever comes across their path, without thinking for a moment whether it is good or bad. Not only that, they train their children in such a way that they too have to suffer when they grow up. Everyone is born with the impressions of innumerable past lives. Over and above that the parents are training their children so that their tendencies go toward worldly enjoyments. Blessed are they who are trying to escape, overcoming these obstacles.

When by God's grace you have escaped from the meshes of the world, be careful that you don't miss the opportunity to realize God. Be up and doing. Hold God firmly. Don't look here and there. Fix your mind only on him. He will take all responsibility for you. Then all worldly desires will leave you forever.

Can anyone realize God with this puny intellect? What power do you have? Surrender to him completely. Let him do what he wants to do. His will be done. Love him. Have intense yearning for him. This whole world is a huge lunatic asylum. If you want to be mad, be mad for God and not for the fleeting objects of the world.

The goal of human life is God-realization and not action. But selfless action is a means to the goal. Practice your disciplines and go forward. Then you will know that God alone is real and everything else is unreal. You might have a little awakening by practicing japam and meditation for some days, but that does not mean you have attained everything. You have to move further. Then only will you realize God and be blessed with his vision. Gradually you will be able to talk to him.

You have studied, argued, and debated on the scriptures long enough. Now collect your scattered mind and focus it on God. Tell your mind, "Please plunge into the ocean of God."

After renouncing hearth and home, if you become involved with petty things and do not dedicate yourself fully to God, you will lose both this world and the next. When through the grace of God you have a good resolve, please make the best use of it. Do not sacrifice the infinite bliss of God for momentary pleasures of the world. Pray to the Lord, "O Master, give me strength and perseverance to overcome all obstacles that stand in my way to you."

All worldly pleasures become insipid to one who has tasted divine bliss. What is there in the world? Wife, children, wealth, name, and fame—none of these can bring peace to anyone. Rather, they increase one's misery and anxiety. Whatever enjoyable things you see around will merge into nothingness as soon as you close your eyes. The path of enjoyment is trying to lead you from darkness to deeper darkness. Do you want to stumble painfully on the path of darkness or walk joyfully on the path of light? When you have gotten a glimpse of the light, do not look again at the alluring, enjoyable things of the world. If you do so, you will be drowned. The influence of enjoyment is so powerful that if it once leaves an impression on your mind, it can drag you down to a lower and still lower plane before you know it. The only way to be saved from these dangers is to offer yourself solely to God. If you are not strengthened by his power, you will not be able to escape from the trap of maya. How can a man comprehend the infinite God? He alone can understand God whom God chooses out of his own mercy. They alone can cut the meshes of maya and attain liberation who have obtained his grace.

33

SURRENDER—THE GURU—GRACE—CONTROL OF THE MIND—RENUNCIATION—FAITH

Place: Belur Math
Year: 1918

MAHARAJ: Complete self-surrender to God is not a trifling matter. These questions naturally arise in the mind: Without knowing God, how can I love him? Without seeing him, how can I surrender myself to him? Once a person said to the Master, "Sir, I don't feel inclined to call on God." "Whom do you love?" asked the Master. "I love my pet sheep." "Very well," said the Master. "When you feed and serve the sheep, think that you are feeding and serving the Lord himself. Do this sincerely for some time and you will find that everything is all right."

It is the guru who shows his disciple the way to cross the ocean of maya and who removes his obstacles. Have faith in the words of your guru and follow what he tells you. You will see that all impurities of the mind will go away and slowly the light of knowledge will dawn from within. You will definitely succeed if you follow your guru with faith. Don't consider your guru to be an ordinary human being. To a disciple the guru is a veritable manifestation of God. There is a verse in the Guru Gita: "The guru is Brahma; the guru is Vishnu; the guru is Shiva himself. Verily the guru is none other than the highest Brahman. Salutations unto the guru."

The Master used to say: "A man's ego is destroyed after three croaks, as it were, if he falls into the clutches of a real teacher. But if the teacher is an 'unripe' one, then both teacher and disciple undergo endless suffering. The disciple cannot get rid of either his ego or the shackles of the world. If a disciple falls into the clutches of an incompetent teacher, he doesn't attain liberation. How is it ever possible for one who has not realized God or received his command, and who is not sustained by divine strength, to save others from the prison of the world?'' If the blind lead the blind, both are sure to come to grief. Only one who is free himself can make others free and show how to attain freedom.

If a person has sincere longing for God and is eager to follow the spiritual path, he is sure to find a real guru through the grace of the Lord. It is not necessary for an aspirant to be anxious for a guru. The spiritual lives of those who have come under the guidance of a real guru are well taken care of. They are on the right track, and now they will have to move on.

The Master said: "The world is like a hog-plum. The hog-plum has only pit and skin, and after eating it you suffer from colic." You are all pure, young souls. Your minds are still under your control and not yet distracted by worldly thoughts. From now on, if you make a little effort you will be able to realize God easily. As long as you are young you can fix your mind on God without much exertion. But it is hard to bring the mind under control in old age when it has become scattered.

There is a beautiful saying of the Vaishnavas [the followers of Vishnu]: "A man received the grace of the three—the guru, the Lord, and the devotees of the Lord. But without the grace of the one [his own mind] that person's life was doomed." You have received the blessing of your guru, and by the grace of God you have a desire for liberation. Besides this you have got the association of holy people. Now what is wanted is the grace of the one, that is, of the mind. When the mind comes under control then only can one realize the grace of the others. The mind must be brought under control at any cost. Unless this is done, all efforts will be in vain.

It is the nature of the mind to move toward sense objects.

For that reason I tell you, be careful! Your mind has not yet learned to wander about. Before it does so, hold tightly to the reins. As a mahout [an elephant driver] trains a huge elephant and then makes it do whatever he pleases, so you will have to train your mind in such a way that it moves according to your direction. Don't let the mind be your master. The only way to discipline the mind is to stop its desires for enjoyment. When this is accomplished the mind will be your slave. That is why the Bhagavad Gita and other scriptures declare again and again the glory of renunciation.

Renunciation, renunciation, renunciation! Without this there is no other way to reach the goal. Only they whose minds are not yet scattered in the world can understand the greatness of renunciation. The Master used to say: "A parrot learns to repeat the holy names of Radha and Krishna when it is young. When it is grown it can only utter its own natural sound 'Kaa! Kaa!'" While you are young you can get a deep impression of God in your mind and can easily follow the spiritual path.

How simple and strong is the faith of little boys! They believe what they are told and try to act accordingly. In whatever direction they focus their undistracted minds they attain success. But with the advance of age there comes a tendency to be skeptical. At last they reach a state where it becomes very hard for them to have faith in anything. Therefore, whatever you want to do, do it right now while you are young. I saw how the Master used to teach renunciation to his young disciples. "The goal of human life is to realize God"—this idea he tried to impress on their minds. He knew that these young disciples would imbibe his ideal fully and carry his message. Fortunately you boys are still young and your minds are not colored with worldliness. This is the right time to give up cravings for the world and dedicate yourselves solely to God.

You cannot have divine bliss and worldly pleasures at the

same time. You cannot get the one without renouncing the other. Once you get the taste of divine bliss, the desire for worldly pleasures will automatically fall away. One who has tasted the syrup of sugar candy cannot enjoy a drink made from common treacle. This is the best time of your life to fill the mind fully with divine thoughts and make God your own. "God is my all in all"—when this idea is firmly fixed in your mind, all troubles will come to an end for you, and no one will ever be able to harm you. Offer this life to God. Let him do with you as he pleases. Surrender, surrender, surrender!

34

THE HOLY CITY OF VARANASI—WATER OF THE HOLY GANGA—THE KUNDALINI

Place: Advaita Ashrama, Varanasi
Date: January 21, 1921

MAHARAJ: What a great influence the holy city of Varanasi has on me! While coming here by car from Mugalsarai, I noticed meadows on both sides of the road. It gave me no joy at all. But as soon as I crossed the bridge over the Ganga and reached Varanasi, I felt an inexpressible joy! This place is the abode of Lord Shiva. Here Mother Annapurna [the goddess of food] is removing the external need of the people by feeding them, and Lord Vishwanath [Shiva] is bestowing spirituality. A bearded, luminous Being appeared once before Sri Ramakrishna. He was Mahakala Bhairav [the guardian deity of Varanasi], and he showed the Master the glory of Varanasi.

It was evening. Swami Brahmananda asked for a little Ganga water to be brought in. He took some himself and then asked others to sprinkle it about. After saluting the Master, the swami said: The water of the Ganga is considered to be the water of Brahman. It has a tremendous purifying power. It helps one to have the vision of the Chosen Deity. The Master used to say, "Ganga water, the prasad [offered food] of Lord Jagannath, and the dust of Vrindaban are pure like Brahman."

PRESENTLY MAHARAJ SAID: When the direction of the kundalini is downward, the mind dwells in the three lower planes—at the navel, at the organ of generation, and at the organ of evacuation, and when it is upward, the mind dwells on God. When the mind has a preponderance of sattva guna, one desires to have the vision of God. Then one enjoys japam and meditation.

35

JAPAM AND PURASHCHARANA—FOOD—METHODICAL DISCIPLINES—MEDITATION

Place: Advaita Ashrama, Varanasi
Date: January 24, 1921

In the morning Maharaj asked one monk: Are your spiritual practices going well?

THE MONK: No, Maharaj. My mind is restless, and I do not get any joy. I don't find any unfoldment within, so I have no peace. Evidently we were born with such bad samskaras that these stand in the way of our spiritual progress.

MAHARAJ: You should not think that way. Practice japam at midnight or early in the morning before sunrise. Perform *purashcharana*.[1] Do not waste time anymore. Absorb yourself in

---

[1] Purashcharana is the performance of japam a certain number of times each day, methodically increasing and decreasing the amount.

prayer and meditation. Let me see you make an effort. How can you expect unfoldment without sadhana?

ANOTHER MONK: Maharaj, I have to eat my supper late, so I feel heavy in both body and mind. As a result I cannot get up early. On the other hand, if I do not eat I feel weak. Please tell me what I should do.

MAHARAJ: Reduce your food intake. At first take three-fourths of your usual diet and then reduce it to half. In the beginning you may feel a little weak, but later your system will adjust and you will feel active and light. During the time of our *tapasya* [austerity] we used to eat one meal a day, and as a result we always felt light.

In the evening Swami Brahmananda was seated in his room with Swami Saradananda. Gradually the monks and brahmacharins assembled there and saluted the swamis.

MAHARAJ (*to a monk*): A spiritual aspirant should ask for instructions from a guru and then follow those instructions methodically. He cannot make any progress if he proceeds in a haphazard way. Again, if he discontinues for a time and then resumes practice, he will have to work doubly hard in order to attain the desired result. Of course his previous effort will not be lost. Lust, anger, and greed gradually go away from one who practices sadhana. Now your mind is covered with *rajas* [restlessness] and *tamas* [dullness]. You will have to make it pure and subtle and raise it to the state of *sattva* [calmness]. Then you will enjoy your japam and meditation, and a desire will come to practice more. Later on, when the mind is fully purified, it will remain absorbed in meditation. The mind is at present on the gross material plane, so it is attracted by material objects. But when the mind dwells in the subtle plane, it will be attracted by God-consciousness. The more subtle the mind becomes, the more its capacity increases and it comprehends the mystery of God.

When you practice meditation, first think of the blissful form of your Chosen Deity. That will soothe your nerves. Think that he is looking at you with a smiling face and with joy. Otherwise your meditation will be dry and tedious. Waste no more time. The senses are very powerful, but they must be kept under control. This is no doubt a troublesome task. Work hard for seven or eight years. Then you will enjoy the fruits of your practices. You will see some results within a year. Even women devotees are practicing austerities, so why don't you? I know a girl here [in Varanasi] who has made tremendous progress within a year, and now she is experiencing bliss. Women have more faith than men so they make quicker progress. Believe me, Sri Ramakrishna is always with you. If you practice a little, the Master will extend his helping hand. He will protect you from all miseries and troubles. How unbounded is his grace! It cannot be described.

Try to experience for yourself what you have heard. One should begin practice according to one's own mode of sadhana. After becoming established in that, one can take up other paths and experience the same bliss of God. Don't be emotional. Control your feelings. Japam becomes tasteless if it is not connected with the thought of the Chosen Deity. If you cannot visualize the full form during meditation, start with only one part. First concentrate on the lotus feet of the Deity. Even if you fail again and again, struggle again and again! Don't give up. Make a firm resolve. Is meditation an easy affair? It comes by repeated practice. After meditation comes samadhi. Self-surrender, the culmination of sadhana, comes from within. Resign yourself wholly unto him.

36

MEDITATION—VISION—BRAHMACHARYA—OBSTACLES—GRACE—HALLUCINATION VS. VISION—THE VALUE OF RITUALS

Place: Advaita Ashrama, Varanasi
Date: January 1921

A MONK: Maharaj, some meditate on the Chosen Deity in the heart and some in the head, but I meditate on my Chosen Deity outside, just as I see you sitting in front of me. Please tell me the proper way.

MAHARAJ: Well, meditation differs according to the different mental attitudes of aspirants. As a general rule, however, it is best to meditate in the heart. Think that your body is a temple and the Master is seated within. When your mind is calm through meditation, you can see your Chosen Deity anywhere. Then you can meditate inside the heart or outside, in front of you or to your side. It will no longer matter.

While practicing meditation an aspirant first sees light. With this vision the mind experiences a kind of joy and does not want to move forward. Then he sees a luminous form and his mind gets absorbed in that. Sometimes the mind becomes absorbed while listening to the long sound of OM. Is there any end to the realm of vision and realization? The more you advance, the more you will realize that this realm is infinite. Some people, seeing a little light, think that is the end, but it is not. Some say it is the end of sadhana when the mind stops functioning, and again some say that it is the beginning.

QUESTION: Maharaj, it often happens that the mind, after making some progress, cannot advance further. Why does this happen?

MAHARAJ: That is the weakness of the mind. The mind has

reached the limit of its capability, and then it is incapable of grasping more. All minds do not have the same capacity. One should strive to increase the capacity of one's mind. The Master used to say, "Brahmacharya increases the power of the mind." Lust and anger cannot perturb a strong mind. They are insignificant to a man of steady mind. He has attained so much self-confidence that passions cannot perturb him. There are many obstacles in spiritual life. For that reason *mudras* [gestures of the hands], purification of the asana and elements, and other practices are prescribed in ritualistic worship.

QUESTION: Maharaj, we get encouraged when you ask us individually about our spiritual progress and difficulties. Please do it often so we can get inspiration from you.

MAHARAJ: But you see, that mood does not come to me all the time. Sometimes I feel like entreating you, even touching your feet, saying, "My son, please do this and do that." And again I think: "What can I do? The Lord exists and everybody is acting according to his will. Whom shall I instruct? God is the cause, the instrument, and everything. Why should people accept my words?" But you see, if God speaks from within, one accepts his words and follows them. Be up and doing. Do not waste time. At the close of each day Sri Ramakrishna used to weep and pray, "Mother, another day is gone and I am not yet blessed with thy vision." Have tremendous longing for God and be absorbed in the thought of him.

QUESTION: Maharaj, is grace conditional?

MAHARAJ: The Master used to say: "To avoid heatstroke, a person uses a fan. But when the gentle breeze starts blowing, he stops fanning." So it is with grace.

QUESTION: How does one know whether one is having a true vision of God or a hallucination?

MAHARAJ: The true vision of God brings lasting bliss, and the mind is aware of its validity.

QUESTION: Maharaj, what is the importance of mudras and

the act of touching different parts of one's body while reciting different mantras during ritualistic worship?

MAHARAJ: Rituals are very helpful in counteracting bad influences on the mind. You might have noticed that sometimes your mind is calm until you sit for meditation, and that it suddenly becomes restless with bad thoughts. Once it happened to me. Seeing me from a distance Sri Ramakrishna understood my condition. As soon as I reached him he said, "I see a worldly thought is disturbing your mind." Saying this, he touched my head and repeated something inaudibly. Within five minutes that worldly thought disappeared from my mind. When the mind reaches the higher plane of consciousness, no bad influence can touch it.

QUESTION: Isn't it extremely difficult to pass the time only in practicing japam and meditation?

MAHARAJ: Why should you give up just because you fail a few times? Try again and again. It becomes easy through repeated practice.

37

WORSHIP—MEDITATION—SAMADHI—THE GURU—
BLISS—THE ABSOLUTE AND THE MANIFESTATION (THE NITYA AND THE LILA)

Place: Advaita Ashrama, Varanasi
Date: February 3, 1921

QUESTION: Maharaj, you talked to us about worship, study, and meditation. Did you mean external worship?

MAHARAJ: Worship means both external and mental worship. In external worship certain articles such as flowers, incense, fruits, and water are necessary. It is sometimes difficult to collect all those things, so mental worship is more convenient for you. Mentally offer flowers, incense, fruits, and water to the Lord, and then mentally repeat the mantram and practice meditation. In mental japam, even the tongue is not supposed to move, but the movement of the lips is permissible while repeating one's mantram during regular sadhana.

In meditation you should think of the form of the Chosen Deity as effulgent. Imagine that everything is shining through his lustre. Think of him as a conscious Being. This kind of meditation gradually turns into meditation on the formless aspect of God. Your awareness will be filled with God-consciousness. Then, when the knowledge-eye [*jnana-cakshu*] opens, you will see God face to face. Oh! That is a different world. Compared to that spiritual world, this material world is nothing. Seeing the grandeur and beauty of Calcutta, Udi [a village boy of Orissa, who was a cook for Maharaj] remarked, "Bhuvaneswar is a poor place."

Gradually the mind becomes absorbed in *savikalpa samadhi* [in which the awareness of the meditator, meditation, and the object of meditation remains] and after that in *nirvikalpa samadhi* [superconscious experience without thought]. The experience of that transcendental realm cannot be expressed by words. In that state there is nothing to be seen, there is nothing to be heard. Everything is merged in the Infinite. It is a matter of experience. Then one has to bring the mind forcibly to the world of phenomena. At that time the aspirant feels this world to be unreal. "The Atman is beyond duality and nonduality." Reaching that state, some regard the body as an obstacle to uninterrupted communion with Cosmic Consciousness, and they cast it off in samadhi. It is like breaking an earthen jar. Sri Ramakrishna explained this through an illustration: "Suppose there are ten pots filled with water, and the sun is reflected in them. You break the pots one after another until one is left with the reflected sun in it. What remains when that last pot is broken? You cannot say that the real sun remains. Who will say so? What remains cannot be described. What *is* remains. How will you know there is a real sun unless there is a reflected sun? 'I-consciousness is destroyed in samadhi.' "

QUESTION: Maharaj, some think of the Chosen Deity as all-pervading. Isn't this also a form of meditation?

MAHARAJ: Yes, quite so. But first one should establish him in one's own heart. Later one can feel his presence everywhere—in water, on land, in leaves and trees, in space and stars, in hills and valleys.

QUESTION: Maharaj, the scriptures say that if you want to know the secret of spiritual life you should give personal service to your guru.

MAHARAJ: Yes, it is necessary in the initial stage, but later the mind becomes the guru. The guru should not be looked upon as an ordinary human being. His physical body is the temple in which the Lord resides. If the guru is served with this attitude, one attains love and devotion for him, which can then be directed toward the Lord. One should meditate on the guru in the thousand-petalled lotus of the brain [*sahasrara*], and then merge the guru into the Chosen Deity. Sri Ramakrishna used to say: "The guru appears before the disciple in a vision and points ahead, saying, 'Look, there is your Chosen Deity.' After this the guru himself merges into the Chosen Deity." Really the guru is not different from the Chosen Deity.

There are so many mysteries in spiritual life. How can I tell you everything? Follow the spiritual path with sincerity. When the mind becomes pure through religious practices, you will understand many things about the spiritual world. You will then remain absorbed in them and can locate the place in the heart where you should concentrate on the Chosen Deity.

QUESTION: Maharaj, it seems to me that if one gets a little taste of divine bliss, one should be able to make rapid progress in spiritual life.

MAHARAJ: What are you saying about bliss? There is no joy or sorrow, happiness or misery, being or nonbeing in that absolute state. An aspirant experiences bliss only during sadhana. The boat needs a favorable wind till it reaches its destination. And once it has reached its destination, the wind is no longer needed. As a favorable wind helps the boat, so bliss helps the aspirant. The knower, knowledge, and the object of knowledge—all three become one with the Absolute. The scriptures describe what happens up to this point. But what takes place after this, none has the power to describe. One can experience that mysterious phenomenon only through sadhana. The Infinite is a matter of personal experience. In that state there is no desire and no fear either. The very thought of it elevates the soul. What great fun it is! Some experience both the *nitya* [Absolute] and the *lila* [manifestation].

QUESTION: Maharaj, first one experiences the Absolute and then the lila. Isn't that true?

MAHARAJ: There is no hard and fast rule about it. For some the reverse is true. During the time of the *raslila* [when Krishna played with the gopis on the full moon night of autumn], one gopi said to another, "Friend, the goal of Vedanta is dancing." The goal of Vedanta is Supreme Brahman—in other words, Sri Krishna. Here the nitya and the lila became one. There is yet another state, which is beyond both the Absolute and the relative.

38

THE KUNDALINI—MEDITATION—CONCENTRATION—THE GRACE OF THE GURU

Place: Advaita Ashrama, Varanasi
Date: February 5, 1921

QUESTION: Maharaj, how can the kundalini be awakened?

MAHARAJ: By practicing japam and meditation. Some say there is a special sadhana to rouse the kundalini, but I believe it awakens through japam and meditation. In this kali yuga [iron age] there is no easier sadhana than japam and meditation. One should practice meditation along with japam.

QUESTION: What is meditation? Does it not mean thinking of the form of a deity?

MAHARAJ: It means thinking of God with form as well as without form.

QUESTION: Maharaj, isn't it the guru who decides whether one should meditate on God with form or without form?

MAHARAJ: Yes. But the pure mind itself plays the part of the guru. Sometimes one loves to think of God with form and sometimes without form. One's human guru is not always available, so one should keep engaged in sadhana, and the pure mind will guide one from within. According to the Yoga-Vashishtha Ramayana [a scripture on Vedanta philosophy], the mind wastes its energy if it moves in various directions. A part of the mind is drawn to the body, another part to the senses, and still another part to the sense objects. Cut all these attachments. Collect the scattered forces of the mind and focus them on God. This is called sadhana. Until you realize God, concentrate the entire mind on him. Work hard. Be up and doing. You are still young. It is extremely hard to do anything in later years. Start your sadhana with zeal and vigor. If you can gather all the scattered powers of the mind, you will find that tremendous energy has been generated. Do something. One can attain perfection either through japam or meditation or discrimination. These three have the same result. Take one of them and dive deep into the spiritual realm. For now, do not question anymore. First do something. Then come and ask questions if you have any.

QUESTION: Maharaj, is it true that the kundalini can be awakened by the grace of the guru?

MAHARAJ: Of course. By the grace of the guru one can attain even the knowledge of Brahman, not to speak of awakening the kundalini. But is it so easy to have the grace of the guru? One has to strive one's utmost to get it. Ask your mind in solitude, "What have I done?" Your mind will answer, "Nothing." Please do something. Dive deep and forget the world. In the beginning it is good to make a routine and then follow it strictly. It does not matter whether your mind likes it or dislikes it. You must practice your japam and meditation as a daily routine.

39

HOW TO ACQUIRE TASTE FOR SPIRITUAL LIFE—STRUGGLE—AUSTERITY—FAITH—SELF-EFFORT—SELF-SURRENDER

Place: Advaita Ashrama, Varanasi
Date: February 1921

QUESTION: Maharaj, I am practicing japam and meditation mechanically and am not acquiring any taste for them. What should I do?

MAHARAJ: Is it possible to get that taste in the beginning? No, it just does not come at the outset. You will have to struggle hard to attain it. Direct all your energy to that one pursuit. Don't keep any other interest. Move onward and forward! Never be satisfied with a little progress. Try to create dissatisfaction in the mind, saying to yourself: "What am I doing? I am not making any progress." The Master used to say: "Mother, another day is gone in vain; still thou art not revealed unto me!"

Every night before you go to bed think for a while about how much time you have spent in doing good deeds, how much you have frittered away doing useless things, how much you have utilized in meditating, and how much you have wasted doing nothing at all. Make your mind strong through austerity and brahmacharya. The duty of a rich man's gatekeeper is to prevent thieves, cows, and other intruders from entering the estate. Likewise, the mind is your gatekeeper. The stronger it is, the better protected you are. The mind has been compared to an unruly horse. Such a horse takes the rider in the wrong direction. Only he who can firmly hold the reins of the horse reaches his destination.

Struggle, struggle on! What are you doing? Do you think it is enough that you have renounced hearth and home and put on an ochre cloth [the garb of a monk]? What have you achieved? Time is running out. Do not waste a single moment. Probably you will be able to practice hard another three or four years, and after that your body and mind will become weak. Then it will be hard for you to do any sadhana. Can anybody achieve anything without labor? If you think that after attaining love, devotion, and faith you will call on God, it will never happen. Light follows the rising of the sun. Similarly, when God appears, then love, devotion, and faith follow him as his retinue.

People practice austerity to know God. Without austerity

nothing can be achieved. In the beginning of creation Brahma [the Creator] first heard, "Tapas, tapas, tapas," which means if you want to know God, practice tapas, or austerity. Don't you see how even the avatars had to go through so many hardships? What tremendous austerities Buddha, Shankara, and Chaitanya practiced! Ah, what burning renunciation they had!

Does anybody achieve true faith in the very beginning? True faith comes from realization. At first an aspirant must have faith in the instructions of his guru or any great soul. Then he must proceed forward. One may call it "blind faith," but an aspirant must have something to hold onto. Do you remember Sri Ramakrishna's parable of the pearl oyster? A pearl oyster floats about on the surface of the sea with its shell wide open. But when it catches a raindrop while the star Svati is in the ascendant, it dives down to the bottom of the sea and makes a pearl out of it. Similarly, you have received a precious mantram from your guru. Now dive deep into the ocean of Satchidananda.

You have no self-reliance. Self-effort is indispensable in spiritual life. Do something for a period of at least four years. Then if you have not made any tangible progress come and slap my face! Japam and meditation are impossible unless you have transcended rajas and tamas and are established in sattva. After that, in order to attain the Highest, from which there is no more return, you will even have to rise above sattva.

How difficult it is to attain a human birth! Humans are the only living beings capable of realizing God. Strive hard in this life to reach that state from which you will not have to come back. The mind is to be raised step by step—from the gross to the subtle, from the subtle to the causal, from the causal to the Great Cause [Brahman], and finally to samadhi [absorption in Brahman].

Surrender yourself fully to the Lord. There is nothing but him. "Verily all this is Brahman." He is all in all, and everything belongs to him. Never calculate. Is it possible to surrender oneself in a day? When surrender is achieved, everything is over. One should struggle hard for self-surrender. Life is eternal. The span of man's life is at the most a hundred years. If you want to enjoy the happiness of eternal life, you will have to give up the pleasures of these hundred years.

40

WORK AND WORSHIP—BRAHMACHARYA—THE SECRET OF WORK—HOW TO CONTROL THE SENSES

Place: Advaita Ashrama, Varanasi
Date: February 12, 1921

MAHARAJ (*to a disciple*): How are you doing with your spiritual practices?

DISCIPLE: Maharaj, there is so much work to do that I don't have enough time to practice my spiritual disciplines.

MAHARAJ: It is a mistake to think that you do not have any time for meditation because of the pressure of work. The real cause is restlessness of the mind. Work and worship must go hand in hand. It is very good if one can devote oneself fully to spiritual practices. But how many can do so? Two types of persons can live in this world adopting the "python method," which means sitting in one place and doing nothing, not even striving for food. One is the idiot who is too dull to be active. The other is the saint who has gone beyond all activity. The Bhagavad Gita says, "Without performing action none can attain that actionless state" [3.4]. One can attain knowledge through the path of action. As we have noticed, even those who give up work and lead a retired life have to spend a great deal of their time in putting up thatches on their roofs, cooking food, and doing other things.

Work for the Lord. If you work with the idea that you work for the Master and Swamiji, the work will not bind you. On the contrary, it will improve you in every way—spiritually, morally, intellectually, and also physically. Give yourself up wholly to Sri Ramakrishna and Swami Vivekananda and be their servants. Pray to them, saying: "Here I am, offering my body and mind to you. Please use them in whatever way you see fit. I am ready to serve you to the best of my ability." Then they will take responsibility for you, and you will not have to worry anymore. But you must resign yourself in the right spirit. It will be hypocrisy if you "chant the Lord's name and lift up your cloth at the same time."[1]

We led a wandering life for five or six years and then became involved in the Master's work. One day Swamiji said to me: "Look, there is nothing in a wandering life. Work for the sake of the Lord." After that we did various kinds of work, and I do not think it did us any harm. We had tremendous faith in Swamiji's words. Have firm faith in the words of the Master and Swamiji and work for their cause. There is nothing to be afraid of. Some may try to confuse you, saying, "The work

---

[1] This is a reference to Sri Ramakrishna's story of a milkmaid who had to cross a river to deliver milk to a priest. She was often late due to an undependable boatman. The priest scolded her, saying: "Men cross the ocean of existence by the name of God. Can you not cross this little river by the same means?" From the next day she was never again late. One day she explained, "Since I cross the river as advised by you, by uttering the name of the Lord, I do not need a boatman." The priest wanted to see for himself. The woman told him to follow her, and she began to walk over the water. The priest tried to follow her but was soon sinking. The woman told him: "You are uttering the name of God, but at the same time you are taking every care to save your cloth from getting wet. You are not fully relying on the Lord."

you have undertaken has nothing to do with Sri Ramakrishna or Swamiji." Don't listen to them. Even if the whole world stands against you, never give up what you believe to be true.

MONK: It is extremely difficult to devote oneself exclusively to spiritual practices. I tried but could not continue for very long.

MAHARAJ: Why do you think that you cannot do it just because you failed three or four times? One has to try again and again. The Master used to say: "When a newborn calf tries to stand it falls a hundred times, but it never gives up. At last it learns to run."

The mind gets good training if one takes up regular work at the beginning of spiritual life. Then that disciplined mind can be engaged in meditation. If the mind is allowed to drift, it will drift at the time of meditation also. There comes a time when an aspirant wants to devote himself solely to meditation and prayer. At that time work falls off from him by itself. This happens when the mind has become spiritually awakened. Otherwise, if one forcibly devotes oneself exclusively to spiritual practices, after a few days monotony comes. Some who have tried to do this have even gone out of their minds. Others practice their disciplines superficially and meanwhile keep their minds busy with other things.

Brahmacharya generates tremendous power. A true brahmacharin can do the work of twenty-five men. In the old days, besides the practice of continence, brahmacharya also included japam, meditation, the study of scriptures, pilgrimage, and having holy company. All people do not know what is good for them. For that reason one should keep the company of one's guru and holy people. If I were to give you freedom to practice sadhana on a full-time basis, how long could you keep it up? Not long—not even a few days. You would have trouble because your mind has not yet been properly trained. There is no enemy more harmful than idle gossip. It completely ruins a person. Unless one spends some time in solitude, one cannot understand the workings of the mind and grasp the Truth. It is hard to grow spiritually in the midst of a hectic life.

Is there any place better than the Himalayas?[2] It is so quiet, serene, and holy! It is the abode of Lord Shiva. The cold climate of the Himalayas keeps the brain calm, and one can accomplish four hours' work in one hour. I give freedom to all. I let everyone move forward according to his own way, but when I see that someone is not able to do so, then I go to his aid.

It is good in every way to remain in one particular center and take up some work of the Master and Swamiji. If you stay in a center without working, you may feel that you are taking food and giving nothing in return. Others also may comment in the same vein. But if you render some form of service each day, you will feel right in both body and mind. We have experienced that. Let me speak of myself just by way of illustration. I am now retired from active work. Some people think that they too should do as I am doing and become less active. Never entertain such a thought.

Eternal life is in front of you. What if you devote a few lives to the cause of Sri Ramakrishna and Swamiji! If it is a mistake to lose a few lives, let it be. But I assure you that will never happen. Through their grace, like a rocket, you will be lifted to the higher realms of spirituality. Do not lead an easygoing life anymore. Meditation is not possible for sluggish people. Swamiji used to tell us: ''Whatever you do, concentrate your whole mind on that. This is the secret of work.''

Now do something. It is not such an impossible task for you to edit a magazine. Before you begin your work, salute the

[2] Maharaj mentioned the Himalayas because that monk was going to Mayavati, Himalayas, as an editor of the *Prabuddha Bharata*.

Master. Remember him at intervals in the course of your work, and again salute him after you finish it. Spend your time in thinking of the lives and teachings of Sri Ramakrishna and Swamiji. Know for certain that you work for them and none else.

Control the mind. Instead of indulging in inertia, learn to stop the thought-waves of the mind. Meditation and japam will automatically help to restrain the senses, but in the beginning you must make an extra effort to control them. The power to practice meditation for a long time in one sitting comes gradually. In the beginning it is good to practice meditation four to five times a day. Whether your mind likes it or not repeat your mantram. The habit of sitting like this will definitely curb the restlessness of the mind. That serene state may come at anytime provided you continue your disciplines even if you don't like them. When the kundalini rises, the senses become powerless. Then one is not even aware of their existence.

41

THE ADVANTAGE OF YOUTH—TRAINING THE MIND— WHERE IS BLISS?—HAPPINESS AND MISERY—THE GOAL OF HUMAN LIFE

Place: Advaita Ashrama, Varanasi
Year: 1921

MAHARAJ: Do you know why I talk to you again and again about spiritual life? When we were young like you, the Master forced us to practice sadhana. In boyhood the mind is soft like clay, and it receives an indelible impression from whatever comes in contact with it. As long as the clay is soft, you can give it any shape you like. But once the clay is baked, no more change is possible. Now your mind is like soft clay. It can still be molded in any shape you want. It is pure and unworldly and can still be easily directed toward God. From now on, if you can engage your mind in thoughts of God, no worldly thought will be able to make an impression. Once the mind becomes steady in God-consciousness, you will not have to worry anymore.

The mind is like a bag of mustard seeds. Just as it is extremely difficult to gather the mustard seeds if they have been scattered on the floor, so once the mind has been scattered in worldly affairs, in later years it is hard to collect it and fix it on God. For that reason I tell you to mold the mind now before it is scattered in mundane things. Otherwise later on you will suffer and experience tremendous difficulty in focusing the mind on a particular object. Whatever you want to do, do it between sixteen and thirty. After that the chances are slim for illumination. Your body and mind are still fresh and energetic. This is the time to set your goal of God-realization and strive for it earnestly. Whatever impression you give the mind during this period of your life will remain with you forever.

Begin your spiritual life right now. If you can put the mind in a spiritual mold, if you can make God the be-all and end-all of your life, if you can devote yourself sincerely to realizing him, your life will take a beautiful shape and no suffering or misery will touch you. You will experience joy and inherit eternal bliss.

What does man want? Bliss. He runs here, there, and everywhere for bliss. He plans for it. He strives for it. But does he get bliss? When he is baffled after many failed attempts, he changes his plan again and again, but to no avail. So his life just ebbs away. His luck is not favorable for procuring bliss. He works his whole life like a coolie, enduring sorrows and sufferings, and at last leaves the world. Vain is his coming and vain is his going. Nothing better can be expected of one who runs after empty pleasures, forgetting the goal of life.

If you want real happiness, you will have to sacrifice all worldly pleasures and all attachments to momentary joys and direct your whole mind to God. The more you advance toward him, the more bliss you will get. And again, the more you are attached to the world and its objects, the more you will suffer.

Do you know the nature of ordinary human beings? They seek pleasures, fun, and frivolities. Young or old, rich or poor—almost all are running after pleasures, but their very attempts are defective. I think ninety-nine percent of them do not know where real happiness and fun are. They grasp whatever they see in front of them, thinking they have found the right thing. When they get blows they take up something else. Thus they go on and on. Look. Here is the tragedy: They are getting blow after blow, but they neither change their direction nor cross over to the right path. The Master used to say: "The camel loves to eat thorny bushes. The more it eats the thorns, the more the blood gushes from its mouth. Still it eats thorny plants and will never give them up." People suffer from untold miseries due to lack of good tendencies, good habits, and good actions. You boys are all young, and your minds have not yet received worldly impressions. If you struggle hard from now on, you will be able to escape life's sorrows and sufferings.

One might have plenty of money, relatives, and friends, but they cannot give permanent happiness. Worldly enjoyment lasts five to ten minutes—half an hour maximum. After pleasure comes pain. Every action must have a reaction. We must aspire for that joy which has no reaction, and that is the joy of God. Except for this divine joy, whatever joy you find in this world has a reaction. And where there is a reaction, there is misery.

Never forget the goal of life. This life is not meant for eating and sleeping like animals and passing our days in idle gossip. The goal of human life is God-realization. When you have got this precious human life, shun the momentary pleasures of the world so you can realize God. Make a firm resolution to experience the Truth. Take a vow: do or die. Why have you come away from your hearth and home in the name of Sri Ramakrishna? If you really want to get rid of the sorrows and sufferings of the world, quickly move toward the goal while your body and mind are strong. Never have the attitude that realization will come in the course of time or by the grace of God. It is a sign of laziness and I do not support it. Why don't you just say in plain language that you still have a desire for enjoyments? Unite your mind and speech.

You are waiting for the right time! Don't you see that the best part of your life—between sixteen and thirty—is passing away? Do you think that after wasting these valuable years in useless pursuits you will be able to take up spiritual practices in your old age? That is self-deception.

42

RELIGION IN OLD AGE—GRACE—FOLLOW ONE PATH— DEMAND FROM GOD HIS VISION—THE RAZOR'S EDGE— BRAHMACHARYA

Place: Advaita Ashrama, Varanasi
Year: 1921

MAHARAJ: Some people spend their lives in worldly affairs and then retire and live on their pensions in a holy place. They think that the holy influence will counteract the results of their bad deeds and that after death they will get liberation. Is it not sheer madness? Of course those who sincerely believe that the holy place has a purifying power, will imbibe some good samskaras and get their results. That is all. But Varanasi is different from other holy places. It is true that a person will get liberation if he dies in Varanasi. Vishwanath [Lord Shiva, the presiding deity of Varanasi] is truly the Lord of the universe, and his play is unusual and incomprehensible. One person attained liberation at the time of death after passing a miserable life, and another person passed his life in japam and meditation and attained the bliss of liberation while living. Of these two who was the wiser? Sri Ramakrishna used to say, "One can enter the house either through the front door or through the back door." Which is better?

Another thing is grace. The breeze of God's grace is always blowing. You only have to unfurl your sail. Give up desires for enjoyment, name, and fame and resign yourself fully to God. Is it ever possible to have both sense enjoyments and God-realization? It cannot be. Choose one. Don't put your feet in two boats. It will be a disaster, and you will suffer. Follow one path.

Now you are all young. This is the right time to select an ideal. If you cannot do it now, it will never be done. God is very close to that person who knows that the Lord is his very own and who has for his sake renounced all desires for enjoyments. Such a man binds God with the ties of love, as Yashoda and the gopis bound Krishna with their love.

Sri Ramakrishna used to say, "He who has renounced everything for God has every right to make demands of him." As one can endearingly make demands of one's parents and relatives, so a devotee has the right to press God for his vision. God answers the sincere prayer of the devotee immediately. He who has been touched by God knows what inexpressible bliss it is! Compared to it, worldly pleasures, so dear to most people, become worthless and insipid. The Master further said, "Those who have shunned sense pleasures for God have already covered three-fourths of their journey." Is it so easy to give up physical enjoyments? Man attains the power of renunciation through the grace of God and through the result of austerities in his previous birth. Train your mind in such a way that carnal desires do not have a chance to rise in it. It is extremely difficult to lead this life. This path is not as easy as you young boys think. Do you know what it is like? It is like walking on the sharp edge of a sword. Every moment there is a chance of being sliced to pieces. Without unbroken chastity it is almost impossible to walk on this path. And again it is very difficult, nay impossible, to maintain brahmacharya without love and faith in God. You have to live in a world full of enjoyments and luxuries. Every day you see before you more than ninety-nine percent of the people madly running about after sense pleasures. As a result there is every possibility that you could receive those worldly impressions in your mind. Once you have that worldly experience, there is very little chance for you.

Those who want to lead the life of a brahmachari must always engage their minds in studying holy books, discussing spiritual life, worshipping the Lord, serving holy people, having holy company, and practicing japam and meditation. This is the way one can mold one's character.

First try to be established in the practice of brahmacharya. Everything else will come by itself. Brahmacharya depends upon spiritual practices and God-realization depends upon brahmacharya. Moreover, human life is meaningless without God-realization. Bliss comes after the vision of God. You are all young boys. You still have fine intellects and pure minds. Just strive a little and you will attain devotion and faith.

43

FORBEARANCE—TRUTH AND A HARSH TRUTH—POWER OF ADJUSTMENT—DREAMS—SRI RAMAKRISHNA'S REBIRTH

Place: Sri Ramakrishna Math, Madras
Date: June 1921

QUESTION: Maharaj, we have come here leaving our hearth and home. But we still have not overcome the perversities of the mind. We are not getting along together.

MAHARAJ: My boy, put up with everything. The Master used to say, "He who endures is saved." Is there anything more noble than living harmoniously with others? How much one must forbear in this world! Can any good come to those who hurt others?

"Tell the truth, tell what is agreeable, but don't tell an unpleasant truth." Never tell a harsh truth if it might hurt someone. Just see how different sorts of people come to me—good and bad—and I receive them all with equal care and courtesy. If bad people come here and are told, "Go away!"—where will they go? Everyone can live with illumined souls like Sanaka and Sanatana. Nobility consists in being able to live with all sorts of people.

QUESTION: Maharaj, are dreams about saintly souls true?

MAHARAJ: Yes, they are very true. Sometimes saints reveal themselves in dreams. Out of mercy they render a great many services in dreams. All dreams about gods and goddesses, the Chosen Deity, and saints are very true. It is better not to tell about these dreams to one and all. Then they make a lasting impression.

QUESTION: Maharaj, I have heard that Sri Ramakrishna will

soon reappear in the region of Burdwan [West Bengal]. Is this true?

MAHARAJ: I have never heard that. I have only heard that he will come again in the region of the northwest.

QUESTION: Maharaj, some say the Master will come again after one hundred years and some say after two hundred years.

MAHARAJ: I know nothing about the time of his coming, nor have I heard anything about it.

44

FIX THE MIND ON GOD—DOUBT AND FAITH—GOD IS BEYOND THE MIND—SAMADHI—THE THREE GUNAS—HOW TO LIVE IN THE WORLD—HOW TO OVERCOME DEPRESSION—FOUR KINDS OF WORSHIP—HOW TO CONQUER BAD THOUGHTS—DETERMINE YOUR IDEAL—THE VALIDITY OF THE SCRIPTURES—ABOUT FOOD—NONVIOLENCE

Place: A devotee's house, Calcutta
Date: February 19, 1922

MAHARAJ (*to a devotee*): How are you?
DEVOTEE: I am all right.
MAHARAJ: How is your mind?
DEVOTEE: Presently it is not bad.
MAHARAJ: That is good. If the mind is fine, everything is fine. Surrender to the Lord, and let his will be done. Divert the mind from the world to God. This world is a painful place. It is best not to give too much attention to it. But this does not mean that you must give up your duties. There are some good qualities within you. If you practice a little, you will make tremendous progress. Struggle, struggle—you will have to

struggle hard. Be up and doing. After practicing a few days you will find how much joy and fun there is in spiritual life. In this very life you will have to transcend the play of maya. It is not an easy task. Strive hard and have unshakable faith. Throw off all doubts from the mind. Hold the truth with all your might!

DEVOTEE: If doubt creeps in at times, what shall I do?

MAHARAJ: One cannot have real faith unless one realizes God and has his vision. But before the aspirant reaches the goal, he comes to a stage where he is convinced of the existence of God. Faith becomes strengthened through repeated practice. Never doubt the existence of God. When doubt arises in the mind, think to yourself: "God *is*. But I cannot see him because of my bad karma and because of the samskaras in my mind. I will have to wait for his grace."

Can this finite mind comprehend the infinite God? He is beyond the mind and the intellect. The creation which you see in front of you is the kingdom of the mind, and the mind is its ruler as well as its creator. The mind cannot go beyond its own creation. Through the practice of spiritual disciplines, though, a subtle mind evolves. That mind is latent in every human being in a subtle seed form. When it is developed through sadhana, one experiences many subtle truths. This, however, is not the final experience. The subtle mind leads an aspirant closer to the Supreme Self, or Brahman, but it cannot reach there. In this stage an aspirant does not relish worldly enjoyments. He longs only to be absorbed in the thought of God.

The next stage is samadhi, which cannot be described. It is beyond "yea" and "nay." In samadhi there is neither happiness nor misery, neither joy nor pain, neither light nor darkness. Human language is inadequate for expressing that blessed and sublime state.

In the Vedanta scriptures we find the three gunas discussed: sattva, rajas, and tamas. Without tran[scending] these three gunas one cannot reach God. Krishna sa[ys in the] Gita: "The Vedas deal with the three gunas. Be free, O Arjuna, from the three gunas" [2.45]. Tamas expresses itself as fighting, killing, envy, jealousy, pride, and ego. Rajas goads human beings into activity and creates the desire for name and fame. A person of rajasic nature meditates for some time and then looks around to see if he has attracted the attention of others. Then comes sattva guna, which is a preponderance of good qualities. Brahman, the Supreme Reality, is devoid of gunas. Therefore, in order to reach Brahman one must go beyond the gunas.

DEVOTEE: How should we perform our worldly duties?

MAHARAJ: Perform your duties without attachment. If you know from the bottom of your heart that this world belongs to God and not to you, then no harm will come to you. Eradicate all feeling of ownership. Never say, "It is mine." Only God knows how long he will keep you in this world and what he will do through you.

Do your duties conscientiously. Let no one doubt your sincerity. But in your heart of hearts you should know that you have nothing. Everything belongs to God. Never be attached to anything. Intensely feel that God is the doer and you are the instrument. Let his will be done.

DEVOTEE: Maharaj, while performing duties according to your instruction, if my mind gets confused or if I feel attachment for any object, what shall I do?

MAHARAJ: Do not yield to depression. Never allow yourself to be depressed. It does not matter if you fail a few times. Try again with redoubled energy. Have tremendous zeal in the mind. Never give up. "Do or die"—let this be your motto.

Make a firm resolution that in this very life you will realize God. Otherwise, what is the use of having this body and mind? Blessed are you if you die in the attempt to realize God!

DEVOTEE: What is the significance of all the gods and goddesses and various kinds of ritualistic worship?

MAHARAJ: All gods and goddesses are only different manifestations of the one Godhead. Men differ in their temperaments, so they imagine all those forms with their minds. To meet the needs of all, the scriptures prescribe four kinds of worship: "The highest worship is to think of oneself as Brahman; the second method of worship is meditation on God; the third method is japam, prayer, and glorification of God; and the last method is external, ritualistic worship."

The highest sadhana is to experience the Atman all the time. The stage prior to this is meditation. At that time the aspirant feels that only God and he exist. In deep meditation he sees the form of his Chosen Deity and cannot continue his japam. In the stage prior to meditation the aspirant glorifies God, chants his name, and at the same time thinks of his form. The last method is the ritualistic worship of God embodied in an image or symbol. These are all different stages of evolution of the mind. Each person begins his spiritual journey from where he is.

Suppose an ordinary man is instructed to meditate on the formless Brahman or to practice samadhi. It is not yet possible for him to understand these things. For a while he may try, but sooner or later he will become frustrated with his failures and give up his sadhana. But if he is asked to worship the Lord with flowers and incense, he will understand at once what to do. He will follow the instructions, and he will get the feeling that he has done something. For a time his mind will be calm and he will get some joy. By and by he will outgrow that stage and go to the next.

The finer the mind becomes, the less it finds pleasure in

gross objects. For example, today you have started ritualistic worship. After a few days you will feel more joy in japam than in worship, and gradually you will begin to feel more joy in meditation than in japam. This is how an aspirant moves toward the highest Goal. This is called natural growth. In the course of this mental evolution, the experiences the mind acquires are not lost.

Suppose you are in the courtyard and you want to go to the roof. Now instead of climbing the staircase step by step, if you are hurled bodily up there, what will happen? You will be seriously injured. One should follow a gradual path. Just as there are laws in the physical world, so there are laws governing the spiritual world.

DEVOTEE: I know some thoughts are very harmful for me. Still, if they persistently arise in my mind, what should I do?

MAHARAJ: Think to yourself: "This thought is immensely harmful to me. It is my enemy and may ruin my whole life." Imprint this idea again and again on your mind. Gradually you will notice that the thought will disappear. Take, for example, this boy sitting here. Now you think about him: "This boy is good for nothing. He is stupid." Before long you will find that you are not drawn to this boy, and that, moreover, he has become insignificant to you. Take another illustration: A little child is not aware of the effect of taking poison, so if there is any deadly poison near him, he is not afraid of it. But if you see it, you are afraid because you know the effects of poison. So you see, this mind is a mysterious phenomenon. Whatever you teach it, it learns accordingly.

First determine your ideal. God is the only ideal of life. Your ideal must not be lowered or compromised. God is "smaller than the smallest and greater than the greatest." He shines forth always and everywhere. He dwells in you as well as in me and also in other beings. It is the same Atman that pervades everything. In some places it manifests more and in some places less. Practice a little meditation. You will find there is a lot of fun in spiritual life. You have seen enough of the worldly side of life. Now see the other side—the real side. "Knock and it shall be opened unto you." A veil is hiding the Reality. Remove that veil and see God. It is not an impossible task to cross the barrier of maya. Become sincerely involved in spiritual life and you will soon find that the whole world is transformed.

DEVOTEE: Is it true what the scriptures say?

MAHARAJ: Yes, it is true. One should abide by the authority of the scriptures, as those injunctions were formulated through the ages for the good of mankind. Follow your karma as enjoined by the scriptures, and this karma will lead you to the goal. Karma is without beginning but it has an end. When you experience the Truth, all your karmas will drop off.

DEVOTEE: What dietary rules should a person follow?

MAHARAJ: It is a very difficult question. And it is hard to answer. People differ widely in their constitutions, so it is not possible to lay down any hard and fast rule about food. One kind of food may agree with my system but not with yours. For this reason the scriptures did not give specific instructions about food. The reference to food in the Bhagavad Gita [17.8–10] is not specific. It gives only a general classification. On the whole it can be said, however, that rich food should be avoided, and that one should choose one's food according to one's power of assimilation.

DEVOTEE: Maharaj, isn't it cruel for a man to eat meat and fish?

MAHARAJ: Nonsense! The scriptures say, "Nonviolence is a great virtue." This experience comes when a person attains samadhi, the knowledge of oneness, and sees God in everything. Until then mere talk about *ahimsa* [nonviolence] is meaningless. You will be established in ahimsa when you realize that the same Atman resides in you as well as in the little ant and that there is no difference between the two of you.

You are talking about nonviolence, but truly speaking, can you avoid violence? What should you eat? Potatoes? Plant a potato underground. It shoots forth young sprouts. Has the potato no life? Should you eat rice? Plant the paddy grain in the ground. It grows into a rice plant. Does it not have any life? You want to drink water? Examine a drop of water through a microscope and see how many millions of tiny lives are there. You must breathe to live, yet with every breath you kill millions of microbes. You don't feel bad killing all these lives, but you think you will lose your religion if you eat a piece of fish! Such an argument is foolish. Don't those who advocate vegetarian food take milk and butter? You drink milk, depriving an innocent calf of its legitimate food. Truly speaking, it is an extremely cruel act. However, these arguments are not rational. The ancient Hindus held no such ideas, but later they were introduced by some religious sects.

45

AUSTERITY—TRUTHFULNESS—LUST—DESIRE

Place: Belur Math
Date: March 17, 1922

It was evening. The vesper service was going on in the shrine of Sri Ramakrishna. The ringing of bells could be heard from different temples situated on both sides of the Ganga. Swami Brahmananda was seated quietly on the verandah. A few devotees were seated in front of him. After an hour the monks and brahmacharins came and saluted the swami one by one and sat down. A devotee also bowed down to him and asked a few questions.

DEVOTEE: Maharaj, what is tapasya, or austerity?

MAHARAJ: There are various kinds of austerity. Some people take a vow that they will not sit for a long period. I met a monk who had taken a vow not to sit for twelve years. At that time he had almost finished that period, having only five or six months left. Due to constant standing his legs had swelled as they do in elephantiasis. Both ends of a rope were tied to a wooden frame, and the monk used to sleep at night holding onto that rope.

There is another type of austerity practiced during winter, when one stands all night up to the neck in very cold water and repeats the mantram. During summer one surrounds oneself with blazing fires and sits under the sun practicing japam. There is another kind of austerity in which one repeats the mantram while standing or sitting on pointed nails.

DEVOTEE: Is that true austerity?

MAHARAJ: Heaven only knows! People practice such austerities with some motive, hoping perhaps that they will be kings in their next life or enjoy all the luxuries of this world to their heart's content.

DEVOTEE: Do they get those results?

MAHARAJ: God only knows!

DEVOTEE: Then what is real austerity?

MAHARAJ: Real austerity is not in performing feats such as those. Anyone can do such things by practice. It is easy to conquer the body, but it is extremely difficult to conquer the mind and its desires for lust and gold, name and fame.

Real austerity depends on three things: First, you must be truthful. Completely establish your life on truth and then perform action. Second, you must conquer lust. Third, you must conquer worldly cravings. Observe these three basic principles. To assimilate them in your life is real austerity. Of these, the second one is most important—conquering lust. Our scriptures say, God-realization is easy for those who have strictly practiced brahmacharya for twelve years. This is very difficult. I am telling you from my own experience that deep meditation is not possible without practicing brahmacharya. It is a difficult task to control subtle desires. That is why there are so many strict rules for monastics. A monk is not supposed to look with lust at women. It is the nature of the mind to enjoy beautiful objects. Unconsciously the mind enjoys many things, and this is harmful to spiritual life. When your life is established in brahmacharya, you will see the manifestation of the Divine in everything. By observing brahmacharya one accumulates *ojas* [spiritual energy] in the brain. But remember, one cannot observe the vow of brahmacharya without practicing japam.

46

ON THE DIVINE NAME

As God is all-powerful, so is his name. Work sincerely and repeat the name of the Lord unceasingly. Connect your mantram with the wheel of karma and you will get the result. All of your sufferings will cease to exist. So many sinners, repeating God's name, have become the pure, free Atman.

Have firm faith in God and in his name. Unite God with his name. God dwells in the hearts of devotees as the mantram [the sound of Brahman].

One should call on God wholeheartedly in solitude. From time to time pray: "Lord, have mercy on me. Give me faith, sincerity, and devotion." Call on him in such an intense way that tears flow from your eyes. Let your thought be one with your speech.

Try to see God in everyone. Humility will come from the practice of the presence of God. Keep the company of the holy and hear only about God. That place is a deserted cremation ground where the name of God is not sung. No evil spirit dares to come near those who repeat God's name.

Call on God. He is your very own. Why will he not reveal himself unto you? Open your heart to him and he will show you the right way. If you need anything, ask him for it. He will fulfill all your desires.

What is initiation? Repetition of the holy name of the Lord. The guru gives the mantram of the Deity whom the disciple loves most. Then it is the duty of the disciple to practice japam and meditation with faith and love.

In the initial stage prayer is beneficial. Call on him, glorify his name, and pray intensely: "O Lord, you are the creator of the sun, the moon, and the universe. You are compassionate, omniscient, and omnipresent. Be gracious unto me. Give me right understanding, faith, love, and devotion."

You might have much work to do, but never forget to practice your spiritual disciplines twice a day. Nothing can purify the body and mind except japam and meditation. The Lord is easily available to his devotees. Make him your very own and dedicate yourself to him. A precious object becomes dear to a person because it is rare. So God is dear to us.

Repeat God's name and listen to his praise. God and the name of God are identical. If you get involved in this world without repeating his name, you will be lost in a maze.

47

ON SADHANA

Practice sadhana with steadfast devotion. Do not miss a single day. Whether you like it or not, sit for meditation on your seat regularly. If you can continue this routine for three years, your love for God will grow. You will develop a natural inclination to call on God, and the outgoing tendencies of your mind will stop. Gradually you will begin to get joy from japam and meditation.

Truly, there is joy in spiritual life. When a person gets the taste of that divine bliss, all worldly pleasures become insipid to him. The joy of meditation does not come in the beginning. You will have to follow the instructions of your guru with faith for some time. Then joy will automatically come.

A true aspirant practices his disciplines under all circumstances. If he finds a favorable place, he devotes more time to practice. But those who complain of lack of time or suitable conditions and who move around like vagabonds, do not make any progress.

Practice japam more and more. In this kali yuga repeating the name of the Lord is the easiest way to realize God. Nowadays it is hard to practice yoga or to perform Vedic sacrifices. Repetition of the mantram will bring calmness of the mind, and gradually the mind will settle on the Chosen Deity. Think of the Chosen Deity while repeating the mantram. Thus one can perform japam and meditation simultaneously and attain quick progress.

Practice constant remembrance of God. Time and opportunity are necessary for practicing japam and meditation, but thinking of God does not depend on anything. One can practice it while eating, sleeping, sitting, or walking. Know for certain that if you can constantly have this recollectedness, your mind will dwell in the higher realm. According to Ramanuja [an exponent of Qualified Nondualism], this uninterrupted flow of thought is meditation.

Take it from our experience, my boys—you won't achieve anything by moving around like vagabonds. Stay in one place and practice your disciplines methodically for some time. Then you will get the result. Swami Vivekananda established such a beautiful monastery where you need not worry about food and clothing. If you want to realize God, dive deep in the realm of spirituality! Otherwise, simply moving around like an itinerant monk, begging for food from door to door, will not help you to realize God if you don't practice sadhana.

One cannot conquer the senses merely by saying: "I shall conquer lust. I shall conquer anger, greed, and so on." If you fix your mind on God, the power of the senses will be reduced automatically. You will not have to make any extra effort. Sri Ramakrishna used to say, "The more you proceed toward the east, the further you are from the west." Call on God and pray to him. Then the senses will no longer be so turbulent.

You practice japam and meditation very superficially. A

couple of hours' practice a day is not enough. You will have to be absorbed in a divine mood day and night. This is the golden period of your life. Dive deep! Dive deep! Do not misuse a single day. Midnight is a very favorable time for practicing japam and meditation. Try to sit at that time.

In the initial stage, you should slowly increase japam and meditation. If today you spend an hour, in a few days add a little more time. Again a few days later devote still more time, and so on. You will suffer from reactions if you practice long hours out of momentary enthusiasm. If this happens, the mind will go to the bottom plane, depression will come, and suddenly you will have no more inclination for japam and meditation. It is an arduous task to raise a depressed mind and turn it back again to sadhana.

Grace is needed. Without God's grace, nothing can be achieved. One should pray to God intensely for his grace. Prayer is very effective. He answers our prayers. Practice every day according to your convenience—even if it is only for five minutes. Night is the best time for meditation. At that time the brain remains cool and is not agitated if you practice for long hours. Moreover, at that time nature is serene, which is favorable for spiritual practice. It is always good to practice meditation in solitude.

48

WORK IS WORSHIP

Motivated by the desire for name and fame, one can perform spectacular work, but in this way one's work cannot be properly appraised. One's day-to-day activities will have to be observed, for it is the ordinary actions of a person which reveal his true character. A real karma-yogi entirely dedicates him-

forms every action as worship, even an ordinary
s never prompted by the least desire for winning
lar applause.

w no cannot do a job if it is of his own choice? Where then lies the difference between a karma-yogi and an ordinary worker? A true karma-yogi knows all work belongs to God, so he welcomes any work that comes his way and gradually adjusts himself to its requirements.

Simply carrying out some undertaking is not sufficient. It must be done in the right spirit, knowing that one is serving the Lord without any motive. Keep three-fourths of your mind fixed on God, and with the remaining one-fourth do whatever you have to do. If you follow this method, you will be an ideal karma-yogi and you will attain peace and joy. On the other hand, if you only get involved with activities without practicing meditation, ego and pride will crop up and quarrels and dissensions will ensue, thus disturbing the equanimity of your mind. Therefore I tell you, stick to your sadhana by all means whether you work or not.

Swami Brahmananda observed that a disciple had just broken a bottle. My goodness! You have broken that bottle! It is a very bad sign. You work with such a restless mind. Why do you think about hundreds of things while engaged in work? No great work—whether spiritual or secular—is possible with an unsteady mind. Whether it is a lofty undertaking or a humble chore, it must be done with concentration. Let me tell you, those who are steady in ordinary work are also steady in their spiritual exercises.

If you want to work in the right spirit, remember these two principles: First, you must have love for the work, and second, you must not seek the results of your work. This is the secret of karma yoga. Always remember, you are working for the Lord. When these basic principles of karma yoga are forgotten, all problems begin and one cannot succeed in either spiritual life or secular work.

Each and every work is equally important—whether it is meditation or household duties. Do it with the right spirit. Work is worship.

The Bhagavad Gita says that man can attain nirvana, liberation, through karma yoga. But it is a difficult path. One needs a cool brain, discrimination, and dispassion to perform karma yoga. Otherwise one drowns in the waves of karma. Truly speaking, it is only after realization that one really becomes fit to perform karma.

49

ON SRI RAMAKRISHNA AND SWAMI VIVEKANANDA

On one occasion Sri Ramakrishna said: "One day as I was meditating in the Kali Temple, I saw in a vision the veils of maya disappearing one after another. In another vision the Divine Mother showed me the light of Brahman, which surpassed the light of even millions of suns together. I then saw that a luminous form emerged from that infinite light and again merged back into its source. I experienced that the formless Brahman took a form and again became formless."

The temple garden of Dakshineswar, which Rani Rasmani had built, provided everything Sri Ramakrishna needed for practicing sadhana. If you have true faith, love, and devotion, God will provide everything you need.

A monk saved ten thousand rupees in a bank. Hearing this, the Master said, "He who calculates pros and cons and plans for the future will ruin his spiritual life."

There is nothing outside. Everything is inside. People are fond of music, but they do not realize that the music we hear with our ears is trivial compared to the music within. How sweet and soothing it is! During his meditation in the Panchavati, Sri Ramakrishna used to listen to the melody of the *vina* [a stringed instrument] within.

Once I was meditating in the Panchavati at noon when the Master was talking about the manifestation of Brahman as sound [*Shabda-Brahman*]. Listening to that discussion, even the birds in the Panchavati began to sing Vedic songs and I heard them.

Sri Ramakrishna used to encourage everybody to practice meditation. A person falls from spiritual life if he does not practice meditation regularly. The Master asked his guru Totapuri, "You have attained perfection, so why do you still practice meditation?" Pointing to his shining brass pot, Totapuri replied, "If you do not clean brass every day, it will be covered with stains." The Master used to say: "The sign of true meditation is that one forgets one's surroundings and body. One will not feel even a crow sitting on one's head." Sri Ramakrishna attained that state. Once while he was meditating in the natmandir, a crow sat on his head.

*   *   *

A great man is born and not made. What bold and prophetic words were uttered by Swami Vivekananda! He said: "Whoever will go and try to imitate me in that land [America] will become bound. He will surely be ensnared." In India, who earned greater name and fame than Swamiji? When he left America he left behind all his costly robes, and on reaching India he put on an ochre cloth like Indian monks. Barefooted, he would go to Calcutta and come back. And like an ordinary man in the public road, he would buy *chanachur* [a mixture of fried grams and nuts] to eat. Sometimes we gave him a pair of shoes to wear and he would accept them. What tremendous fame and honor he earned, but he possessed the power to digest that honor and glory. He used to move around like an insignificant person. The pomp and luxury of the West could not corrupt his mind at all. That is why it is said, a great man is born, not made.

50

MISCELLANEOUS TEACHINGS

It is extremely difficult to practice spiritual disciplines in solitude. You must have love for God and dispassion for the world. In the beginning there is every possibility of falling if you try to live by yourself. For that reason it is better to have a companion. Two people who have similar natures and interest in spiritual life can help each other. If there are more than two persons together, however, it becomes a club. Then they indulge in gossip, which is very injurious to spiritual life. The mind becomes scattered on all sorts of worldly matters and forgets God.

*   *   *

To tell a lie is a great sin. A drunkard or a man who frequents houses of ill fame may be trusted, but never a liar. To lie is the blackest of all sins in this world.

*   *   *

Do not find fault with others or criticize them. Such a habit is harmful to yourself. By thinking day and night of the bad qualities of others, those same qualities will be imprinted on your mind and eventually your good qualities will be wiped out. It is not your business to go poking your nose into others' lives. Follow your own path and reach the goal. Try to see others' good qualities. If you find a little good in a person, magnify it, appreciate it, and respect it. This will make you free from narrowness and jealousy. He is truly a great person who sees greatness in others.

* * *

Never neglect a person no matter how sinful he may be. Give him your love, make him your own, and guide him in overcoming his weaknesses. Good and evil are in every human being. It is easy to see evil in others, but he is a holy man who can overlook their evil qualities and help them to become good and holy.

* * *

The heart must be purified. The whole world is filled with fear. Spiritual life is full of struggles. Subdue the subtle enemies such as lust, anger, and greed. At every step you will have to control your worldly desires, for otherwise they will certainly ensnare you. Pray silently and strengthen your willpower. Gradually everything will become favorable for you.

* * *

Samadhi is of two kinds: savikalpa and nirvikalpa. In savikalpa samadhi one experiences the mystic vision of divine forms without losing one's individual consciousness. What a shame that people are busy with trifling, mundane things and do not practice samadhi! God is your very own. Realize him. In nirvikalpa samadhi one experiences cosmic consciousness transcending name and form. In this samadhi one loses one's individuality and the whole universe disappears. Swami Vivekananda attained nirvikalpa samadhi at Cossipore garden house. He had tremendous control over himself, so very few people knew about it. Besides these two there is yet another kind of samadhi called *ananda samadhi,* or blissful samadhi. If an ordinary person experiences this samadhi, his body and mind cannot withstand that upsurge of bliss, and his *prana* [vital breath] departs from his body through the crown of his head [*Brahma-randhra,* or the passage of Brahman]. One cannot live more than twenty-one days after attaining ananda samadhi.

*   *   *

The human body is the greatest temple of God. For that reason the scriptures suggest practicing meditation within the body. During meditation, when the mind reaches the *sahasrara* [the seventh and highest center of consciousness], it is extremely difficult to bring it down. What is in the microcosm is in the macrocosm. The scriptures say, "When one sees the Lord in the chariot, there is no more rebirth for him." This means that if you experience the Supreme Being in the heart, you will not have to be born again. The external temple, image, chariot, and so on, are for ordinary human beings. When Saint Ramprasad saw the Divine Mother within, he composed this song: "Mother, you have been awakened in my heart, but maya is stealing away my mind and senses." What a wonderful idea! When a person tastes that bliss, he loses all taste for worldly things. Sri Ramakrishna used to say: "In between the eyebrows there is the eye of knowledge [*Jnana-netra,* or the third eye]. When it opens, one experiences bliss all around."

*   *   *

A king dwelt in a palace beyond seven gates. Once a poor man requested the king's minister to allow him an audience with the king, and his request was granted. At each gate sat a man endowed with great power and glory, and at each gate the poor man asked the minister, "Is he the king?" Each time the minister answered, "No." Thus, after passing through seven gates, when the poor man saw the real king with his gorgeous dress and costly ornaments, he was overwhelmed with joy. This time he did not have to ask, "Is he the king?" Similarly, the guru accompanies the disciple step by step on the spiritual journey until the disciple becomes one with God.

Your mind is the greatest guru. When the mind becomes purified and calm through meditation, it will direct you from within. Even in day-to-day activities this inner guru will guide you and continue to help you until you reach the goal. Have intense love and devotion for God, and your mind will be calm and pure.

*   *   *

It is difficult to practice religion if these three powers—physical, mental, and spiritual—are not united. Is God-realization so easy?

*   *   *

Work incessantly and at the same time remember God. Without faith none can realize God. If you have faith, then a copper penny will have value for you, and if you don't have faith, then even a gold coin will have no value. The minds of those who do not have faith in God vacillate, but all doubts disappear from the minds of those who have faith.

*   *   *

Without dispassion for the world one cannot have devotion for God. Dispassion is absolutely necessary in spiritual life. Renunciation means annihilation of the ego.

*   *   *

Only a fanatic says: "My path is right and your path is wrong. If you do not worship my God there is no salvation for you." Human beings with their puny intellects make judgements about right and wrong. Do not judge. Do not quarrel. First realize God, and then you will understand the truth. Let each person follow his own path. There should not be any objection to that.

*   *   *

Some say the mind has two courses—downward and upward. When the mind moves downward the result is jealousy, selfishness, hatred, passion, greed, and laziness. And again, when the mind moves upward one becomes endowed with love, faith, devotion, and unselfishness. Some say the mind has three levels—tamas, rajas, and sattva. Tamas enhances laziness, dullness, and ego. Rajas increases the desire for good food, luxury, name, and fame. Sattva intensifies faith, love, and devotion for God. These levels of the mind are true. We see examples in every step of our life.

*   *   *

There are two paths: the path of devotion and the path of knowledge. A devotee loves God with form. He communicates with God by visualizing his form and by prayer, songs, and tears. On the other hand, a follower of the path of knowledge loves to see the Light—that is, the formless God. Both paths lead in the end to the same goal. Both devotion and knowledge have the power to destroy ignorance. As at the advent of light, darkness disappears, so at the dawn of knowledge, ignorance goes away. Nobody can say what is beyond knowledge. Only that person knows who has experienced that transcendental state.

* * *

A time comes to an aspirant when he does not get satisfaction outside, and yet he feels a void within. He then desperately begs God to fill the emptiness of his mind. This intense longing is the prerequisite for God-realization.

* * *

Is there any greater virtue than charity? The Old Testament says, "Cast thy bread upon the waters, for thou shalt find it after many days" [Ecclesiastes, 11.1]. Whatever you give away as charity will come back to you. Is charity an insignificant matter? All religions speak highly of charity, but one should be very discreet about it. Before you give away your hard-earned money, you should consider carefully whom you are giving it to, what the purpose is for which the money will be used, and so on. Give charity only to an honest person and for the right cause.

* * *

While living in the palace, Buddha saw a monk, a sick person, an old man, and a dead body. He then left the palace to save human beings from birth, disease, old age, and death. After practicing severe austerities he attained nirvana, which is similar to the liberation of the Hindus.

* * *

Pray from the bottom of your heart: "O Lord, you are my very own, so why don't I see you? You are more than my father, mother, brother, friend, and relative. Where are you, Lord? Shall I not see you in this life? I have none else but you to call my own. I beg you for your grace and vision."

What else shall I say? May all good come to you. May your

minds be absorbed in God. Pray to him, talk to him, and establish a relationship with him.

51

A LETTER TO A DISCIPLE

Bhadrak, Orissa
1915

My dear A.—,

I am glad to learn from your letter that by the grace of the Lord you have a desire to spend some time in sadhana and have a convenient place in which to do it. Make the best use of this opportunity. Do not waste your valuable time. Instead of bothering yourself with big metaphysical problems, devote yourself to sadhana. Have faith and work hard. You will not achieve anything without steady practice. Now that all conditions are favorable, please follow your disciplines for at least a year. Gradually your body and mind will become pure, and you will experience many things through God's grace.

I want you to be absorbed in God for some time without doing or thinking of anything concerning the world. Practice japam and meditation, and have constant recollectedness of God. Do not indulge in idle talk or in giving gratuitous advice to others. This is the time to make progress, while your body is still strong and your mind is free from worldly impressions. If you cannot shape your mind now, it will be extremely difficult to do so later. Be up and doing. Pray to God wholeheartedly. He will answer all your questions from within. I shall answer your questions as best as I can. If you follow the routine I suggest for some days, you will get the result.

QUESTION: How many hours a day should one spend in japam

and meditation, and how many in worship and scriptural study?

ANSWER: Devote as much time as possible to japam and meditation and to worship and study. Those who want to lead a purely contemplative life should spend at least sixteen hours a day in japam and meditation. As you continue your practice, you will be able to increase the time. The more the mind is turned inward, the more joy you will get. Once you get joy in meditation, it will be hard to discontinue it. Then you will no longer have to ask how long you should meditate. Your mind will tell you.

Before you reach this stage, try to spend two-thirds of the day in japam and meditation, and the rest of the time in study of the scriptures and self-introspection. It is not enough to practice meditation closing the eyes for an hour. One should examine the mind and eliminate its subtle cravings for the world. Then when the mind becomes calm, one can get deep meditation. The goal of spiritual practices is to calm the mind. If your mind is not tranquil and if you do not get joy within, remember, you are not on the right track. I shall remind you of one thing: The person who is providing food for you will get some result of your sadhana. Therefore you must acquire enough so that you will have some left after giving to others.

QUESTION: Sometimes the mind does not want to practice meditation. What should I do then? Should I occupy myself in the study of the scriptures, or should I force myself to meditate?

ANSWER: It is the nature of the mind to rebel against effort and to always seek comforts. If you want to achieve something you will have to work hard. In the preliminary stage in order to cultivate a strong habit, you must force your mind to meditate. If you find it difficult to sit for long hours, lie down on your bed and practice japam. If you feel sleepy, walk and repeat the mantram. In this way the habit will be formed. Never give up your sadhana. You must wage war against the mind. To bring the mind under control is the goal of spiritual disciplines.

QUESTION: Is it necessary to practice pranayama [breath control], asana [yogic postures], and cleansing processes of hatha yoga [physical exercises]?

ANSWER: At present no such practices are necessary for you. Repeat the name of the Lord, pray to him, and think of him. Believe me, the Lord will make you do whatever is best for you.

QUESTION: How much time should one devote to sleep?

ANSWER: Ordinarily for a healthy person four hours' sleep is quite sufficient. Some may need one or two hours more. To sleep more than five hours is a disease. Too much sleep does not give the body rest. On the contrary, it does harm to the body. It is not good for an aspirant to waste time in sleep. You are young. This is the best time to train the mind. Later you will get plenty of time to sleep.

So often when a person is asked to practice sadhana, he immediately raises a number of lame excuses. He says that his body will not be able to bear such strain, that he needs more rest, and so on. Such an insincere person seeks only rest and comfort without doing anything. If one practices japam and meditation sincerely, one's senses and nerves move in a very rhythmic way, and as a result, four hours' sleep is sufficient. Generally most people lead irregular lives and their bodies and minds are so tired they do not get rest even after eight or ten hours' sleep. Try to regulate your life like a clock. Regulation will keep the body and mind fresh. Do something! What will you gain by only asking questions if you do not practice what I say?

QUESTION: What rules regarding food should I observe? Should I eat whatever I am given or should I discriminate about it?

ANSWER: During sadhana it is better to have a little discrimination about food. Some kinds of food increase sleepiness and should be avoided. It is not good to eat too many sweets, sour pickles, or urad lentils. These foods increase tamas in the body, which means more laziness and more sleep. It is almost impossible for a man of tamasic nature to practice sadhana.

Eat that food which is easily digestible. Never fill your stomach more than two-thirds with food. This will increase your strength and energy. If you overload your stomach, most of your energy will be consumed in digesting the food. Moreover, gas will form in the abdomen, and this will make you uncomfortable. But this will not happen if one third of your stomach is empty. A healthy body is very helpful for sadhana.

QUESTION: Should one observe the vow of silence during this period of intense sadhana?

ANSWER: Forced silence and wild indulgence in talk are equally harmful. It is better to silence the mind than the mouth. The purpose of silence will be served if you do not talk unnecessarily. Moreover, forced silence has many bad effects.

QUESTION: How much clothing should a spiritual aspirant have?

ANSWER: You should have enough clothing to protect yourself from heat and cold. As you are a monk, it is not good for you to collect a lot of clothing and carry it in a bundle. You should not accept anything extra, even if somebody offers it to you. On the other hand, your goal is God-realization and not hardship. An aspirant cannot concentrate on God if he suffers from too much heat or cold. Wear enough clothing to maintain your good health. Procuring many things for enjoyment is luxury, which is extremely dangerous for monastic life. It is terrible to beg for luxurious things from people.

QUESTION: I have no power to do anything by myself. Bless

me that I may have faith in Sri Ramakrishna and in you. Bless me that I may understand your grace and have it always.

ANSWER: Never lose faith in yourself. Sri Ramakrishna will do everything favorable for you. Know for certain it is the Master's will that that gentleman is helping you. Have faith in Sri Ramakrishna and repeat his name. He will reveal the truth to you. Do not be restless. Have patience and go on struggling. You will reach the goal. Do not waste time in useless thinking and metaphysical speculations. God's grace is bestowed on all. One can receive it through sadhana.

I have answered all your questions. Now try to apply these teachings in your life. Please convey my greetings to the gentleman who is helping you to practice your sadhana. He must be a true devotee of God.

Pray to Sri Ramakrishna that you may not have any desire for name and fame.

May the Lord fulfill your good intention and endow you with right understanding.

Your well-wisher,
Swami Brahmananda

Belur Math

APPENDIX

Marble Image of Swami Brahmananda at Belur Math

THE GURU*

In the present age we find religious movements more or less everywhere. Even highly educated Westernized people are turning away from atheism and taking part in some religious movement or other. Among religious inquirers we find people of different natures. Some say: "Follow the traditional customs, be initiated by the hereditary guru, tell your beads, and perform religious austerities. Then you are sure to realize God. One should not forsake one's hereditary guru. It is a great sin to do so. Therefore, no matter what this guru's character is like, be initiated by him and perform spiritual disciplines to the best of your capacity." They themselves follow the same method. Sometimes they read or hear the Mahabharata or the Puranas, and some of them go through the Tantras also.

There are some again who study the scriptures by themselves. Nowadays translations of the Gita, the Puranas, the Upanishads, the Vedanta Sutras, the Yoga philosophy, etc., have been published. With the help of these books, or sometimes with the assistance of a pandit [scholar], they try their best to get at the real essence of the scriptures. From these scriptures they select some method of spiritual practice which suits their temperament, and they practice accordingly. They do not acknowledge the utility of having a guru, or if they acknowledge it they do not think it to be absolutely necessary. Some again do not give any serious thought to it. And among them there are some who say: "If you cannot get a *siddha guru* [i.e., one who has realized God], it matters little whether you have one or not. When we find such a guru we will accept

This is a translation of an article written by Swami Brahmananda in Bengali. It was published in Udbodhan, *Vol. 5, no. 5.*

him as our teacher." Some among these associate with holy men, and some do nothing at all.

"God is omniscient. He will surely hear if you pray to him. He will give you whatever you want, so what is the need of an external guru?"—this is the opinion of a few others. Again, those who hold the opposite view say: "Nothing can be attained without a guru, but any guru will not do. A siddha guru is necessary." Those who are initiated by their hereditary guru and are performing religious practices according to the custom—if they are asked about their progress, they invariably reply that they are merely following their guru's instructions and do not know whether they are progressing or not. "Have you attained peace of mind?" "No, not yet," is the reply. Moreover, it is seen that their love for God is not increasing day by day. The attraction they have for lust and gold—not even an iota of that do they have for God.

From these conflicting opinions the question arises whether a guru is essential in any way for one's liberation or for leading a religious life. If so, then is he an absolute necessity—i.e., is it impossible to attain liberation without a guru? And again, what are the signs of a true guru? To answer these questions we must depend on reason, scriptural testimony, and the sayings of sages.

First let us see what reason says in this matter. A little thought will help us to understand that though prayer and other spiritual practices depend on individual efforts, the world has never seen a person who, just after being born, immediately went to some lonely place and became absorbed in meditation. Many people understand this. For no one is foolish enough to deny that by reading the scriptures and other books and by hearing various religious discourses from pious persons, he has been able to form some idea about God and religion. Even those who doubt the absolute necessity of a guru most likely would not deny that by associating with a holy person, by passing long hours with a sage, and by observing him, one advances spiritually. Nor would they doubt that by seeing a monk's earnest devotion in prayer, his benevolent actions, and other qualities, a desire to possess those noble qualities would arise in a person.

Perhaps they question why one should pay respect to a single individual and follow his teachings forever. In reply to this it may be said that no matter what branch of knowledge a person may study, he needs a teacher at some time or other. It is not that one cannot learn anything without external help, but it takes a longer time, and one has to undergo a good deal of suffering and trouble. One has to learn first what one's forefathers learned and then, if possible, acquire something more—this is the rule. Acquiring knowledge from others does not mean getting by rote what others have to say, but it means making an intelligent study through self-effort. To learn something from others means to make it one's own. This is also true in the case of a spiritual teacher. If we can establish a strong spiritual relationship with an illumined person, then it becomes easy for us to assimilate the truths that he has realized.

Moreover, an advanced guru possesses a special power through which he can understand the spiritual nature of his disciple. Thus he is able to point out to the disciple the easiest way to realize God. If there is any way for the disciple to live with his guru constantly, then the latter can help him, even up to the last moment, by instructing him how to overcome all sorts of obstacles that may arise during sadhana. And further, he can teach the disciple higher and higher methods of spiritual practice according to his progress.

It is the opinion of those who have been blessed by a true guru that there is a great difference between the initiation by a true guru and that by an ordinary hereditary guru. A true guru imparts a special spiritual power with the mantram during the initiation and gives a mantram according to the spiritual nature of the disciple. As a result, by comparatively less effort and sadhana the aspirant attains the goal.

True gurus do some additional service to their disciples. They, in fact, take responsibility for their disciples. If by chance a disciple goes astray, the guru employs various means, both worldly and spiritual, to get him back to the right path. In case any disciple, after acquiring a perfect knowledge of all his guru's teachings, seeks higher realization, then he is at liberty to go to another more advanced guru. But unless the disciple is really advanced it is better that he stick to one guru for life. Otherwise he cannot be firmly established in his ideal. Regarding obedience to the guru, it may be said that a true guru never commands unjustly.

It is necessary to observe a teacher for a long time before accepting him as a true guru. One should not accept anyone and everyone as a guru on the spur of the moment. Those who are desirous of following a true guru should live with him for some time and examine his character until they are convinced that he is a true holy man.

Some may say, "If I have the capacity to judge a true guru then I myself am a guru." But this is not logical. Do you not distinguish good from evil at every step? If you are devoid of that power of judgment, why do you call some things good and some things evil? If you do not have the power of judging a person's character—to find out whether or not he has conquered lust, anger, etc., whether or not he has great devotion and wisdom and is uncovetous, then you should sit in a corner in solitude and with folded hands pray to God, "O God, give me the power of judging good and evil." Some people feel cheated because they take a person to be perfect without examining him thoroughly. But once you have accepted someone as your guru, why should you hesitate to carry out his instructions in every respect? Can he ever lead you to evil?

It is now clear that they alone who have not in the least derived any benefit from being initiated by the hereditary guru and who are really eager to realize God are at liberty to accept a true guru. If it so happens that after becoming initiated by a true guru it becomes impossible to associate with him, either because he has passed away or because he is living in a far off place, then one may take help from any other great teacher without giving up the method of sadhana one has already learned from one's guru. It is said that the Avadhuta[1] accepted twenty-four secondary gurus.

Now let us see what the scriptures say about this. It is not possible to discuss the subject of the guru fully in the light of the scriptures in this short article. Here I shall quote a few passages from the *shruti* [Upanishads], which are the fountainhead of all authority:

"In order that he may understand that eternal Brahman, let him, fuel in hand, approach a guru who is well versed in the Vedas and always devoted to Brahman." [Mundaka Upanishad, 1. 2. 12]

"A man who has found a teacher to instruct him obtains the true knowledge." [Chandogya Upanishad, 6. 14. 2]

"Many there are who do not even hear of the Atman; though hearing of It, many do not comprehend. Wonderful is the expounder and rare the hearer; rare indeed is the experiencer of the Atman taught by an able preceptor." [Katha Upanishad, 1. 2. 7]

"The Atman, when taught by an inferior person, is not easily comprehended, because It is diversely regarded by disputants. But when It is taught by him who has become one

---

[1] Bhagavatam, Book XI, Chapters 7–9.

with the Atman, there can remain no more doubt about It. The Atman is subtler than the subtlest and not to be known through argument." [Katha Upanishad, 1. 2. 8]

"If these truths have been told to a high-minded person who feels the highest devotion for God, and for his guru as for God, then they will surely shine forth [as inner experiences]." [Shvetashvatara Upanishad, 6. 23]

There are also many such passages in the Tantras which discuss the qualifications of a true guru and who is a false guru. The entire purport of all of these scriptures is that realization can be attained only by performing sadhana under the guidance of a true guru. But in some places in the scriptures, statements like, "Whatever be your hereditary guru, be initiated by him"—are also found. These are no doubt later interpolations by the gurus after they had become degenerate and selfish. Religion is not a social matter, so there should not be any mutual obligations and formalities in it. The hereditary guru—i.e., he who was my father's guru—may have the claim to be honored socially, and if I am able I may give him sufficient money also—that much and no further. But when that sincere restlessness for God-realization arises in the heart, where shall I go then except to that place where my yearning will be satisfied? To whom shall I go in search of water but to one who can quench my thirst? I must have the freedom to choose my own guru.

The great sages, when asked, say: "By learning the methods of sadhana from a guru who has realized God, being advised by him at every step, being enlightened at every step by the light of truths realized by him, we have come to this state. If you really want to realize God, you also have to follow the same method." All great people hold the opinion that only a true guru can say what is Real and what is unreal. It

THE GURU

is seen that wherever there is a marvelous manifestation of any religion, a great man is behind it. People in ordinary parlance say, "This man's power is due to the blessings of his guru."

We have read in the scriptures that there is a God, people say that there is a God, but a true guru says, "I have seen God." He also shows his disciple the way to realize God and leads him slowly toward the goal. The very sight of a real guru arouses a loving feeling in the disciple for him. From his very appearance one can see that he has tasted divine bliss and that he is getting more and more absorbed in it as days go on. As soon as one goes near him all sorrows and miseries of the world leave and all worldliness vanishes from the mind. When by his touch the hidden power of Brahman is awakened, the disciple sees an ocean of bliss on all sides.

What can a disciple not do for such a guru? Is it not natural for a disciple to be grateful to him? "Know your guru to be Brahman," say the scriptures. Can such a sentiment arise regarding a professional guru? But it is natural in regard to one who has realized God. Those who bring forth such childish arguments as that it is blasphemy to regard a man as God and they are therefore not inclined to regard the guru as Brahman, and who, due to ignorant dualistic views, imagine an infinite gulf between the Creator and the created—we advise such people to read and understand carefully the Advaita Vedanta and to practice sadhana along with it.

No question can arise as to whether this guru is a brahmin or a shudra, a Hindu, a Mohammedan, or a Christian, a monk or a householder. He who knows Brahman is a guru.

I have seen many gurus in this world and have also taken advice from them, but to no purpose, because they bore no testimony of having known Brahman. Their worldly attachment had not gone. They had neither discrimination nor renunciation. To take advice from an ordinary guru is as fruitless as to ask a blind man for the direction of a place. They cannot impart spiritual power with their advice.

I have heard and I also believe that an illumined guru can empower his disciple through a mantram which can transform the latter's whole life. From the very day of his initiation he begins a new life with renewed faith. I received so many instructions from ordinary gurus, but none has left any impression on my heart. I heard a story on this subject from Sri Ramakrishna:

Once a king felt dispassion for the world. He heard that King Parikshit had attained supreme knowledge by listening to the Bhagavatam for seven days, so he sent for a pandit and began to hear him read the Bhagavatam. The king heard it daily for two months, but he did not attain knowledge of Reality. Then the king asked the pandit, "Why could King Parikshit get supreme knowledge after hearing the Bhagavatam for only seven days, whereas I have gained nothing though I have been hearing it for two months?" He told the pandit that if he failed to give a satisfactory explanation by the next day, he would not get any remuneration whatever.

The pandit returned home very sad. He was afraid of the displeasure of the king, but even after much reflection he could not think of a reply to the king's question. He was greatly troubled and lost in thought. Now he had an intelligent and very devoted daughter. Seeing her father so depressed she asked him to tell her the cause of his sorrow. At last, moved by her affection, he told her what the king had said. The girl laughed and said: "O Father, do not worry. I will give a proper reply to the king."

The next day the pandit appeared at the king's court with his daughter and said to the king, "My daughter will answer your question." The girl then addressed the king, saying, "If you want to have the answer you must do what I say." The king consented, and the pandit's daughter ordered the sentries to bind her as well as the king to two pillars. With the king's approval they did so. Then the girl said, "O King, release me from this bondage." "What nonsense you are saying!" replied the king. "I myself am in bondage. How can I release you?" The girl laughed and said: "O King, this is the reply to your question. King Parikshit was an earnest seeker after liberation, and the teacher was no other than the all-renouncing, illumined, knower of Brahman—Shukadeva. Hearing the Bhagavatam from Shukadeva, King Parikshit attained supreme knowledge. But my father is very attached to the world and is reading the Bhagavatam to you in order to get money. How can you get that wisdom by hearing the Bhagavatam read by him?"

From this story it is clear that there is no chance of our being free from bondage without being guided by a true guru.

We have heard a few other remarks on this subject. Some people say, "No matter what the disciple is like, if he can get a true guru he is sure to attain liberation." Others say, "No matter what the guru is like, the disciple attains liberation if he possesses faith, love, and devotion." We do not deny either of these views, but such cases are very rare in this world. As a general rule both the guru and the disciple should be fit people.

We see many differences among the disciples of the same great person. The teachings are manifest in the disciples' lives according to their merit. If a disciple possesses devotion, humility, and perseverance, he can easily assimilate the teachings of his guru. Our scriptures have clearly delineated the relationship between the guru and the disciple as well as their respective duties. If a disciple follows these duties, he will attain mastery over his body and mind and eventually perfection.

Nowadays we hardly find genuine devotion to the guru. Many people seem determined to do away with it, as they consider it to be hero worship. If this devotion to the guru becomes extinct, then all good qualities such as love, esteem, faith, steadfastness, etc., will surely vanish and license will reign in society in the name of freedom. You may examine a person before you accept him as your guru, but once you have accepted him you must prepare your mind in such a way that at a word from him you can sacrifice everything.

Many persons think that if we depend on the guru to such an extent we will lose our freedom and gradually become like jellyfish. There is no ground for such an apprehension. A true guru never curbs the freedom of his disciple. Rather, he teaches the disciple how to attain freedom, how to stand on his own feet, how to fly like a free bird, cutting all bondages of the senses, mind, family, and society.

How grateful a person feels for a little financial or physical help from others! Why then do you think it unnecessary to show your gratefulness to your guru, from whom you have come to know the purpose of life and who has helped you to achieve the highest bliss?

GLOSSARY

adharma—irreligion; unrighteousness; what is contrary to one's duty in life.

Advaita—nonduality. Also, the name of a school of Vedanta philosophy which teaches the oneness of God, the soul, and the universe. The main exponents of Advaita Vedanta were Gaudapada and Shankara.

ahimsa—noninjury; abstaining from harming other beings by thought, word, and deed.

anahata chakra—the fourth center of consciousness in the human body, located in the region of the heart.

ananda samadhi—blissful samadhi.

anima—one of the eight yogic powers. Anima is the power to make oneself very small.

Annapurna—a name of the Divine Mother. Vishwanath Shiva and Annapurna are the presiding deities of Varanasi.

arati—the waving of light before a deity.

asana—posture. Also, a prayer rug.

Atmananda, Swami—a monastic disciple of Swami Vivekananda.

Avadhuta—a type of sannyasin, or monk. The term often refers specifically to a monk mentioned by Sri Krishna in the eleventh book of the Bhagavatam, who had twenty-four upagurus, or secondary teachers.

avatar—an Incarnation of God.

avidya—ignorance, cosmic or individual, which is responsible for the nonperception of Reality.

Balaram Mandir—the house of Balaram Bose, a householder disciple of Sri Ramakrishna. The Master and his devotees spent many joyous occasions there. On May 1, 1897,

Swami Vivekananda inaugurated the Ramakrishna Mission in this house.

Belur—the village in which the headquarters of the Ramakrishna Math and Mission is located. It is about four miles north and across the Ganga from Calcutta.

Bhagavad Gita—lit., the "Song of God." One of the most important scriptures of the Vedanta philosophy, the Bhagavad Gita, or Gita for short, consists of the teachings of Sri Krishna to Arjuna on how to realize God while carrying on the duties of life. The eighteen chapters of this work are actually a part of the Indian epic, the Mahabharata.

Bhagavatam—one of the more well-known Puranas, or devotional books of the Hindus. The Bhagavatam is especially popular among the Vaishnavas for its stories of devotees and life of Sri Krishna.

bhajans—devotional songs.

bhakti—devotion to God.

Bhakti yoga—the path of devotion. One of the four main yogas, or paths to union with God.

Bhaskarananda, Swami—a famous nineteenth-century holy man who lived in Varanasi.

bhava samadhi—a state of ecstasy in which the sole modification in the mind is the consciousness of one's relationship with God.

Brahma—God in his aspect as the Creator of the universe. The First Person of the Hindu Trinity, the other two being Vishnu and Shiva.

brahmacharin—a celibate student who is dedicated to the study of the scriptures and to the practice of spiritual disciplines.

brahmacharya—continence; abstention from lust in thought, word, and deed. Also, the stage of life in which one lives as a celibate student, devoted to spiritual practices and religious study.

Brahman—the Absolute. The supreme reality of Advaita Vedanta.

Brahma-randhra—lit., "the passage of Brahman." An aperture in the crown of the head. If one's prana, or vital breath, departs from the body through the Brahma-randhra, one is not reborn.

brahmin—a member of the priestly caste, the highest caste in Hindu society.

Brahmo Samaj—a socio-religious reform movement of India, founded by Raja Rammohan Roy (1774–1833).

Buddha—lit., "the Enlightened One." The word refers specifically to Gautama Buddha, 6th century B.C. Born as Prince Siddhartha in what is now Nepal, he renounced the world to become one of the greatest spiritual teachers of all time and the founder of Buddhism.

Chaitanya, Sri—1486–1533. A great saint of Bengal who stressed the repetition of the name of God as a spiritual practice. He is considered by some to be the Incarnation of both Sri Krishna and Sri Radha.

chakra—a center of consciousness. There are six chakras located in the sushumna channel of the spine, and a seventh center is located in the cerebrum. The kundalini, or spiritual energy, lies at the base of the sushumna. When awakened it passes through the first three chakras—the muladhara, the svadhishthana, and the manipura. When the kundalini rises to the fourth chakra, the anahata, in the region of the heart, the aspirant feels the awakening of Divine Consciousness and sees light. At the fifth center, the vishuddha chakra, one likes to hear and talk only about God. When the kundalini rises to the sixth chakra, the ajna, located between the eyebrows, one sees the form of

God, but a little separation remains. The culmination of spiritual life occurs when the kundalini reaches the seventh center, the sahasrara, in the brain. A person then realizes his oneness with God.

Chandi—a book of hymns in praise of the Divine Mother and describing her feats in rescuing her devotees. It is also called Devi Mahatmyam and is a part of the Markandeya Purana.

Chosen Deity—that aspect of the Personal God which a guru instructs a disciple to meditate on in order to attain illumination.

Dakshineswar—a village on the Ganga, about five miles north of Calcutta. Sri Ramakrishna lived in Dakshineswar for thirty years.

dharma—religion; righteousness; one's duty in life, determined by one's nature and tendencies.

Divine Mother—God in the aspect of Mother of the universe.

Ghosh, Girish Chandra—1844–1912. Famous Bengali dramatist and householder disciple of Sri Ramakrishna.

Gita—*see* Bhagavad Gita.

gopis—cowherd girls of Vrindaban, who were companions and devotees of Sri Krishna.

Goswami, Rupa—one of the main disciples of Sri Chaitanya. Rupa and his brother Sanatan were ministers of a Moslem ruler of Bengal. Coming under the influence of Sri Chaitanya, they left their posts and went to Vrindaban. Besides restoring Vrindaban as a place of pilgrimage for its associations with Sri Krishna, they also wrote many works establishing Sri Chaitanya's philosophy.

guna—lit., "quality." Prakriti, or nature, is constituted of three gunas—sattva, rajas, and tamas. When the gunas are in perfect balance there is no creation or manifestation of Brahman. When the balance is disturbed, creation occurs.

Sattva is the quality of balance or wisdom, rajas of activity or restlessness, and tamas of inertia or dullness.

guru—the spiritual teacher. *Gu* means darkness, and *ru* means destroyer. He who destroys the darkness, or ignorance, of the disciple is a guru.

Guru Gita—a hymn on the greatness of the guru in the Vishwasara Tantra.

Hari—another name of Sri Krishna.

hatha yoga—a regulated course of physical and breathing exercises to develop the strength and powers of the body.

Holy Mother (Sri Sarada Devi)—1853–1920. The wife of Sri Ramakrishna. After Sri Ramakrishna passed away she continued the spiritual ministry which he began.

ida—a channel of sensory and motor fibers on the left side of the spinal cord.

Jagannath—lit., "Lord of the universe;" a name of Krishna; the presiding deity of Puri, along with his sister, Subhadra, and his brother, Balaram.

Janaka, King—an ideal king of Hindu mythology, who was established in the knowledge of Brahman yet remained in the world, carrying on his royal duties.

japam—repetition of a mantram, or name of God.

jnana-cakshu—the divine eye of knowledge; the "third eye."

jnana-netra—same as jnana-cakshu.

jnana yoga—the path of knowledge and discrimination. One of the four main yogas, or paths to union with God.

Kali—a name of the Divine Mother. Kali is the deity of the main temple in the Dakshineswar temple garden that was built by Rani Rasmani. Sri Ramakrishna lived there for many years and was priest at that temple.

kali yuga—*see* yuga.

kalpataru tree—the wish-fulfilling tree. On January 1, 1886, Sri Ramakrishna became a kalpataru to many of his householder disciples at the Cossipore garden house when he blessed them, saying, "Be illumined." January 1 is annually observed as Kalpataru Day in the Ramakrishna Order.

Kamarpukur—the village where Sri Ramakrishna was born on February 18, 1836. It is sixty miles northwest of Calcutta.

karma—action which yields results to the doer, or which is the effect of his previous deeds. Also, the sacrificial actions ordained by the scriptures.

karma yoga—the path of selfless work. One of the four main yogas, or paths to union with God.

Krishna, Sri—one of the most widely worshipped Incarnations of God in Hinduism. Sri Krishna delivered the message of the Bhagavad Gita to his friend Arjuna on the battlefield of Kurukshetra.

kundalini—the spiritual energy which lies in a dormant state at the base of the spine. By the practice of yoga the kundalini awakens and rises through the sushumna. Various spiritual experiences occur as the kundalini passes through and arouses each of the chakras, or centers of consciousness.

lila—the divine play or sport of God. Also, the relative plane, consisting of time, space, and causation, in which God himself assumes all the roles out of play. In his special manifestation he becomes the avatar, or Divine Incarnation.

Mahabharata—attributed to Vyasa. The Mahabharata is the longest epic in the world. It describes the conflict and eventual war between the five sons of King Pandu and their cousins, the hundred sons of King Dhritarashtra, over the kingdom. Sri Krishna, who takes the side of the five Pandavas, plays an important role in the drama. The eighteen chapters of the Bhagavad Gita are a part of this epic.

Mahakala Bhairav—the guardian deity of Varanasi.

Mahamaya—the great shakti, or power, of Brahman. The Mother of the universe. She veils a person's vision of Brahman, the Reality, and she projects the manifold universe, making the One appear as many.

Maharaj—lit., "great king." A title of respect used in India when addressing a monk. The term is also used specifically in the Ramakrishna Order to refer to Swami Brahmananda.

mahout—a driver of an elephant.

mantram—a sacred word, verse, or Vedic hymn. Also, the name of God which a guru gives to a disciple at the time of initiation.

Mathur Babu (Mathur Nath Biswas)—son-in-law of Rani Rasmani, the owner of the Dakshineswar temple garden, and devotee of Sri Ramakrishna.

maya—a term of the Vedanta philosophy denoting ignorance which obscures the vision of Reality. Also, the cosmic illusion on account of which the One appears as many, the Absolute as the relative. The word is also used to denote attachment.

Mayavati—a Vedanta center in the Himalayas started in 1899 under the inspiration of Swami Vivekananda. It is the headquarters of Advaita Ashrama, a branch of the Ramakrishna Order, and the editorial office of the journal, *Prabuddha Bharata*.

mudra—a gesture of the hand or hands used during ritualistic worship.

Nag Mahashay (Durga Charan Nag)—a householder disciple of Sri Ramakrishna. He was greatly revered for his extreme renunciation, humility, and devotion for God.

natmandir—a hall or building in front of a shrine, used for spiritual discourses, religious plays, or the singing of devotional songs.

Niranjanananda, Swami—1863–1904. A monastic disciple of Sri Ramakrishna, who was regarded by him as an Ishvarakoti, i.e., one who is eternally free and born on earth for the good of the world.

nirvana—final absorption in Brahman, or the All-pervading Reality, through the annihilation of the individual ego, desire, and passion. It also means liberation.

nirvikalpa samadhi—the highest state of samadhi, in which the aspirant realizes his total oneness with Brahman.

nishkama karma—work performed without any desire for result.

nitya—the Absolute; the ultimate reality.

ojas—energy which has been accumulated through the practice of brahmacharya, and which is stored in the brain.

Om—sometimes written Aum. The most sacred word of the Vedas. It is a symbol of both the Personal God and the Absolute.

Panchatapa—lit., five fires. A spiritual austerity in which four fires are set up in four corners, a certain distance apart—or sometimes a complete circle of fire is made. The aspirant sits in the center, from sunrise to sunset, meditating or repeating a mantram, with the sun (the fifth fire) above.

Panchavati—a grove of five sacred trees—the ashvattha, the banyan, the bel, the amalaki, and the ashoka—in which a person sits for meditation and other spiritual disciplines. Sri Ramakrishna planted a panchavati grove at the Dakshineswar temple garden.

Parikshit—grandson of Arjuna. The Pandavas installed him as king when they renounced their throne. In order to prepare King Parikshit for his death, Shukadeva recited the Bhagavatam to him in seven days, after the king learned that he was cursed to die in that length of time for offending a hermit.

Parvati—the consort of Shiva. A name of the Divine Mother.

Patanjali—the author of the Yoga Sutras and the founder of the Yoga system, one of the six systems of orthodox Hindu philosophy. The Yoga system emphasizes control of the mind, concentration, meditation, etc.

Personal God—God with attributes, as opposed to the Impersonal Absolute. God as the Creator, Preserver, and Destroyer of the universe, who is worshipped and adored by the devotees.

pingala—a channel of sensory and motor fibers on the right side of the spinal cord.

prana—the vital breath, which sustains life in a physical body. Also, the primal energy, or force, of which other physical forces are manifestations.

pranayama—control of the vital energy through the practice of breathing exercises. The fourth of the eight steps in raja yoga.

prasad—food or any other gift which has been offered to God or to a holy person. It is usually distributed afterward to devotees.

Puranas—lit., "ancient." Sacred books of the Hindus which popularize the worship of mainly either Shiva or Vishnu. There are eighteen major Puranas. While dealing with such topics as the creation of the world, the geneology of gods and goddesses, and the dynasty of kings, they also give stories of saints and devotees.

purashcharana—the performance of japam a certain number of times each day, methodically increasing and decreasing the amount.

Radha—the main gopi in Vrindaban, whose ecstatic love for Sri Krishna was regarded by Chaitanya to be the highest form of love for God.

rajas—the principle of activity or restlessness. One of the

three qualities, or gunas, which comprise the universe of mind and matter.

Rama—an Incarnation of God and the hero of the Indian epic, the Ramayana.

Ramakrishna, Sri—1836–1886. A God-man of India, whose life inspired the modern renaissance of Vedanta. After practicing intense spiritual disciplines and realizing his union with God through various paths within Hinduism, as well as through Christianity and Islam, Sri Ramakrishna proclaimed, "As many faiths, so many paths."

Ramakrishna Math and Mission—a twin institution established in the name of Sri Ramakrishna. The nucleus of the Math (lit., "monastery") was formed by Sri Ramakrishna himself, and the Mission (philanthropic activities) was started by Swami Vivekananda in 1897. There are hundreds of branches of the Ramakrishna Order all over the world, including 12 in the U.S.A.

Ramakrishnananda, Swami—1863–1911. A monastic disciple of Sri Ramakrishna. While other monastic disciples went on pilgrimages, he remained at the monastery, steadfastly maintaining a headquarters for their Order. In 1897, at the command of Swami Vivekananda, he went to Madras to establish a center there.

Ramananda, Rai—15th century. A great devotee of Krishna and the governor of the province of Vidyanagar, in South India. Sri Chaitanya met him while on pilgrimage in the South and had illuminating discussions with him.

Ramanuja—1017–1137. A great saint and philosopher of India and the chief exponent of Vishishtadvaita Vedanta, or Qualified Nondualism.

Ramlala—a name of the child Rama. Sri Ramakrishna was initiated into the worship of Ramlala by a monk named Jatadhari, who also gave him an image of Ramlala. Within a few days Sri Ramakrishna began to see the child Rama playing constantly by his side.

Ramnam—a series of songs on the glory of Rama.

Ramprasad—1723–1803. A Bengali poet and saint who wrote hundreds of mystical songs on the Divine Mother.

raslila—lit., "the sweet play of the Lord." The dance Sri Krishna did with the gopis on a full-moon night in autumn.

sadhana—spiritual disciplines practiced by an aspirant.

sahasrara—the highest of the seven centers of consciousness. The sahasrara is located in the cerebrum and is visualized or symbolized as a thousand-petalled lotus.

samadhi—the superconscious state in which a person experiences his identity with the ultimate reality. According to Patanjali, it is a state in which "the true nature of the object shines forth, not distorted by the mind of the perceiver."

samskara—an impression or tendency created in the mind of a person as the result of an action or thought. The sum total of a person's samskaras, including those from previous births, forms his character.

Sanaka—one of the first four offspring of Brahma, the Creator, the other three being Sanatana, Sanandana, and Sanatkumara. They were so pure that as soon as they were born they turned their minds to meditation on God and hence could not continue the creation.

Sanatana—one of the first four offspring of Brahma, the Creator. *See* Sanaka.

Satchidananda—Absolute Existence, Absolute Consciousness, and Absolute Bliss. A term used to describe Brahman, the ultimate reality.

sattva—the principle of calmness and purity. One of the three qualities, or gunas, which comprise the universe of mind and matter.

sattvic—having the nature of sattva.

savikalpa samadhi—a superconscious state attended with self-consciousness in which the mind takes the form of Brahman and rests on it, but does not completely merge the distinctions between the knower, knowledge, and the object of knowledge.

Sen, Keshab Chandra—1838–1884. A well-known lecturer and leader of the Brahmo Samaj, a socio-religious reform movement in India during the nineteenth century. Keshab visited Sri Ramakrishna many times.

Shabda-Brahman—Brahman manifested as the causal sound, especially expressed by the syllable *Om*.

Shakti—the power of Brahman in its functions of creation, preservation, and dissolution of the universe, personified as the Mother of the universe.

Shankara, also Shankaracharya—688–720. A great saint and philosopher of India and the foremost exponent of Advaita Vedanta, or Nondualistic Vedanta.

Shiva—God in his aspect as the Destroyer of the universe. The Third Person of the Hindu Trinity, the other two being Brahma and Vishnu. He is also worshipped as the supreme reality.

Shiva Mahimnah Stotram—"Hymn on the Greatness of Shiva," attributed to Pushpadanta.

shruti—the knowledge which has been learned through hearing, i.e., the Upanishads.

Shuddhananda, Swami—1872–1938. A monastic disciple of Swami Vivekananda. In 1938 he became the fifth president of the Ramakrishna Order.

shudra—a member of the fourth, or lowest, caste of Hindu society.

Shukadeva—the son of Vyasa and the narrator of the Srimad Bhagavatam. He is regarded in India as an ideal monk.

sushumna—a channel in the spinal column extending from the base of the spine to the brain. It is flanked on the left by the ida and on the right by the pingala. When the kundalini, or spiritual energy, is awakened it rises through the sushumna, passing through the various centers of consciousness, or chakras.

Swami—a title of address of a Hindu monk.

tamas—the principle of inertia or dullness. One of the three qualities, or gunas, which comprise the universe of mind and matter.

tamoguna—same as tamas.

Tantras—religious scriptures said to have been revealed by Shiva and which are in the form of a dialogue between Shiva and his consort, Parvati. Many of the Tantras deal with spiritual practices and ritualistic worship in which Shakti is the main deity.

tapas—austerity or spiritual discipline.

tapasya—same as tapas.

Trailanga, Swami—?–1887. An extraordinary saint from South India who lived most of his life in Varanasi. Sri Ramakrishna met him while on a pilgrimage there.

turiya—lit., "the fourth;" the superconscious state. It is called the fourth state of consciousness in relation to the waking, dreaming, and dreamless sleep states.

Turiyananda, Swami—1863–1922. A monastic disciple of Sri Ramakrishna. He came to the United States in 1899 along with Swami Vivekananda and soon after established the Shanti Ashrama, a retreat in the San Antonio Valley of northern California. He returned to India in 1902.

upaguru—subsidiary, or secondary, teacher.

Upanishads—the sacred scriptures which contain the philosophical aspect of the Vedas. The Upanishads mainly deal with the knowledge of God and record the spiritual experiences of the sages of ancient India. There are about one hundred and eight Upanishads, of which eleven are considered major.

Vaishnava—a worshipper of Vishnu, especially in one of his Incarnations such as Rama, Krishna, or Chaitanya.

Vaishnavite—same as Vaishnava.

Varanasi—a sacred city on the Ganga in the north central part of India. It is believed that anyone who dies there is immediately granted liberation and does not have to be reborn. The city is also known as Benaras, Benares, and Kashi.

Vedanta—lit., "the end of the Vedas." One of the six systems of orthodox Hindu philosophy, based mainly on the teachings of the Upanishads, the Bhagavad Gita, and the Brahma Sutras.

Vedanta Sutras—also called Brahma Sutras. An authoritative treatise on the Vedanta philosophy, ascribed to Vyasa. The Vedanta Sutras interpret the spiritual experiences described in the Upanishads through reasoning.

Vedas—the most sacred scriptures of the Hindus and the ultimate authority of the Hindu religion and philosophy. The four Vedas are the Rig Veda, the Sama Veda, the Yajur Veda, and the Atharva Veda.

vidya—knowledge. Also, knowledge leading to the realization of the ultimate reality.

Vidyasagar, Iswar Chandra—a great nineteenth-century philanthropist and reformer of Bengal. Sri Ramakrishna once went to his home to see him.

Vishnu—God in his aspect as the Preserver of the universe. The Second Person of the Hindu Trinity, the other two being Brahma and Shiva. He is also worshipped as the supreme reality.

Vishwanath—an aspect of Shiva worshipped in Varanasi.

Vishwanath and the Divine Mother Annapurna are the presiding deities of Varanasi.

Vivekananda, Swami—1863–1902. Also referred to as Narendra, Naren, and Swamiji, the foremost disciple of Sri Ramakrishna. After the Master's passing away Swami Vivekananda led the monastic disciples in forming the Ramakrishna Order and in spreading the message of Vedanta throughout the world.

Vrindaban—a small town on the bank of the Yamuna River in North India. Sri Krishna spent much of his childhood in Vrindaban with the cowherds.

Vyasa—compiler of the Vedas and author of the Brahma Sutras, the Mahabharata, the Srimad Bhagavatam, and other Puranas. Also, he was the father of Shukadeva.

Yashoda—Krishna's foster-mother, who brought him up in Vrindaban.

yoga—the union of the individual soul with the Supreme Soul. Also, the discipline by which such union is effected. The Yoga system of philosophy, ascribed to Patanjali, is one of the six systems of orthodox Hindu philosophy and deals with the realization of Truth through concentration, meditation, etc.

Yoga-Vasishtha Ramayana—a nondualistic scripture in which the sage Vasishtha gives spiritual instructions to Rama emphasizing the illusoriness of the world.

yuga—according to Hindu cosmology the duration of the universe is divided into four yugas, or ages. The first three, which have already elapsed, are satya (or krita), treta, and dvapara. The present age is the kali yuga. With each successive age human beings deteriorate physically and morally by one quarter.

SUGGESTIONS FOR FURTHER READING

Chetanananda, Swami. *Swami Adbhutananda: Teachings and Reminiscences*. St. Louis: The Vedanta Society, 1980.

Dattatreya Avadhuta. *Avadhuta Gita*. Translated by Swami Chetanananda. Calcutta: Advaita Ashrama, 1984.

M. *The Gospel of Sri Ramakrishna*. Translated by Swami Nikhilananda. New York: Ramakrishna-Vivekananda Center, 1984.

Satprakashananda, Swami. *Meditation: Its Process, Practice, and Culmination*. St. Louis: The Vedanta Society, 1976.

Shivananda, Swami. *For Seekers of God*. Translated by Swami Vividishananda and Swami Gambhirananda. Calcutta: Advaita Ashrama, 1975.

Virajananda, Swami. *Towards the Goal Supreme: Paramartha Prasanga*. Calcutta: Advaita Ashrama, 1979.

Vivekananda, Swami. *Bhakti Yoga*. Calcutta: Advaita Ashrama, 1983.

Vivekananda, Swami. *Inspired Talks*. New York: Ramakrishna-Vivekananda Center, 1987.

Vivekananda, Swami. *Jnana Yoga*. Calcutta: Advaita Ashrama, 1980.

Vivekananda, Swami. *Karma Yoga*. Calcutta: Advaita Ashrama, 1984.

Vivekananda, Swami. *Meditation and Its Methods*. Edited by Swami Chetanananda. Hollywood: Vedanta Press, 1976.

Vivekananda, Swami. *Raja Yoga*. Calcutta: Advaita Ashrama, 1982.

Vivekananda, Swami. *Vedanta: Voice of Freedom*. Edited by Swami Chetanananda. New York: Philosophical Library, 1986.

Yatiswarananda, Swami. *Meditation and Spiritual Life*. Bangalore: Sri Ramakrishna Ashrama, 1979.